WORLD HIS

THE
VIETNAM WAR

A controversial conflict

By Tamra B. Orr

Portions of this book originally appeared in *The Vietnam War* by Hal Marcovitz.

LUCENT
PRESS

Published in 2020 by
Lucent Press, an Imprint of Greenhaven Publishing, LLC
353 3rd Avenue
Suite 255
New York, NY 10010

Designer: Andrea Davison-Bartolotta
Editor: Diane Bailey

Library of Congress Cataloging-in-Publication Data

Names: Orr, Tamra, author.
Title: The Vietnam War : a controversial conflict / Tamra B. Orr.
Description: New York : Lucent Press, [2020] | Series: World history |
  Includes bibliographical references and index.
Identifiers: LCCN 2018042884 (print) | LCCN 2018043735 (ebook) | ISBN
  9781534567849 (eBook) | ISBN 9781534567832 (pbk. book : alk. paper) | ISBN
  9781534567146 (library bound : alk. paper)
Subjects: LCSH: Vietnam War, 1961-1975. | Vietnam War, 1961-1975–Political
  aspects.
Classification: LCC DS557.7 (ebook) | LCC DS557.7 .O77 2020 (print) | DDC
  959.704/3–dc23
LC record available at https://lccn.loc.gov/2018042884

Printed in the United States of America

CPSIA compliance information: Batch #BS19KL: For further information contact Greenhaven Publishing LLC, New York, New York at 1-844-317-7404.

Please visit our website, www.greenhavenpublishing.com. For a free color catalog of all our high-quality books, call toll free 1-844-317-7404 or fax 1-844-317-7405.

Contents

Foreword

History books are often filled with names and dates—words and numbers for students to memorize for a test and forget once they move on to another class. However, what history books should be filled with are great stories, because the history of our world is filled with great stories. Love, death, violence, heroism, and betrayal are not just themes found in novels and movie scripts. They are often the driving forces behind major historical events.

When told in a compelling way, fact is often far more interesting—and sometimes far more unbelievable—than fiction. World history is filled with more drama than the best television shows, and all of it really happened. As readers discover the incredible truth behind the triumphs and tragedies that have impacted the world since ancient times, they also come to understand that everything is connected. Historical events do not exist in a vacuum. The stories that shaped world history continue to shape the present and will undoubtedly shape the future.

The titles in this series aim to provide readers with a comprehensive understanding of pivotal events in world history. They are written with a focus on providing readers with multiple perspectives to help them develop an appreciation for the complexity of the study of history. There is no set lens through which history must be viewed, and these titles encourage readers to analyze different viewpoints to understand why a historical figure acted the way they did or why a contemporary scholar wrote what they did about a historical event. In this way, readers are able to sharpen their critical-thinking skills and apply those skills in their history classes. Readers are aided in this pursuit by formally documented quotations and annotated bibliographies, which encourage further research and debate.

Many of these quotations come from carefully selected primary sources, including diaries, public records, and contemporary research and writings. These valuable primary sources help readers hear the voices of those who directly experienced historical events, as well as the voices of biographers and historians who provide a unique perspective on familiar topics. Their voices all help history come alive in a vibrant way.

As students read the titles in this series, they are provided with clear context in the form of maps, timelines, and informative text. These elements give them the basic facts they need to fully appreciate the high drama that is history.

The study of history is difficult at times—not because of all the information that needs to be memorized, but because of the challenging questions it asks us. How could something as horrible as the Holocaust happen? What are the roots of the struggle for peace in the Middle East? Why are some people reluctant to call themselves feminists? The information presented in each title gives readers the tools they need to confront these questions and participate in the debates they inspire.

As we pore over the stories of events and eras that changed the world, we come to understand a simple truth: No one can escape being a part of history. We are not bystanders; we are active participants in the stories that are being created now and will be written about in history books decades and even centuries from now. The titles in this series help readers gain a deeper appreciation for history and a stronger understanding of the connection between the stories of the past and the stories they are part of right now.

SETTING THE SCENE: A TIMELINE

1941 ········· 1946 ········· 1954 ········· 1964 ········· 1968 ········· 1973

Japanese forces attack the naval base at Pearl Harbor, Hawai'i, and the United States enters World War II; Ho Chi Minh, a Communist, establishes the Viet Minh force to fight for Vietnamese independence.

Cease-fire declared in Vietnam War; all U.S. troops withdraw from Vietnam.

Viet Minh defeat French at battle of Dien Bien Phu; Geneva peace conference splits Vietnam into two countries; and the Vietnam War, or Second Indochina War, begins.

Tet Offensive; Communist forces suffer major defeat, but the battle convinces U.S. political leaders to find a way to withdraw American troops.

U.S. Congress passes Gulf of Tonkin Resolution after North Vietnamese gunboats fire on a U.S. Navy ship.

First Indochina War begins; Viet Minh battle French occupiers in war for independence.

1975 · · · · · · · · **1994** · · · · · · · · **2000** · · · · · · · · **2007** · · · · · · · · **2011** · · · · · · · · **2016**

The United States lifts its ban on selling weapons to Vietnam.

U.S. president Bill Clinton eases economic sanctions on Vietnam, permitting U.S. companies to do business in the Communist nation.

President Bill Clinton goes to Vietnam for a three-day visit.

Vietnam and the United States begin a joint operation to clean up contamination from Agent Orange used during the war.

Vietnam becomes a member of the World Trade Organization; President Nguyen Minh Triet comes to the United States—the first Vietnamese head of state to visit since the end of the war.

South Vietnam falls to the Communists.

THE LONGEST WAR

Humans have always pursued large goals such as power and freedom, but they are rarely achieved quickly or peacefully—if at all. Over the centuries, countless wars have been fought to attain such goals. These wars have shaped the physical boundaries of various countries. They have also shaped the lives of millions of people—both those who went through them and those who were born into societies still struggling with the aftermath.

The Vietnam War, which lasted from 1954 through August 1975, had a profound influence not only in Vietnam, but also in the United States, which officially entered the war in 1964. During this period, more than 1 million Vietnamese were killed or wounded. Another million fled the country and became refugees. After the United States became involved in the conflict, almost 60,000 Americans lost their lives,

The country of Vietnam is long and thin, with most of its cities located on the coast.

and more than 304,000 were wounded. Even as the U.S. government continued to send more soldiers to fight in the war, an anti-war movement began growing throughout America. Finally, in 1973, the U.S. military withdrew from Vietnam, in hopes that a cease-fire agreement would bring an end to the war. Instead, the North Vietnamese army invaded South Vietnam. The battle raged on, but now it was without U.S. soldiers on the front lines. The painful lessons learned during the Vietnam War continue to affect American foreign policy today.

From Allies to Foes

The Vietnam War was closely tied to the larger conflict of the Cold War. The Cold War was not an actual military confrontation. Instead, it referred to a period of icy relations and intense competition involving the United States, the Soviet Union, and their various allies. During World War II, which lasted from 1939 to 1945, the United States and the Soviet Union were allied, but tensions between the two superpowers grew after the war. They began competing for control in dozens of nations in Europe, Asia, Africa, and South America.

During this postwar period, America focused on stopping the spread of Communism into other countries, while the Soviet Union did just the opposite. American leaders tried to strengthen the democracies of countries such as Turkey, Greece, Guatemala, Taiwan, and Indonesia. In other places,

notably China, Communists succeeded in gaining power. In 1949, a Communist regime took power in China. These Chinese Communists became key players in the Cold War, serving as occasional but wary allies of the Soviets.

For more than 40 years, until the Soviet Union's collapse in 1991, the Cold War affected life in virtually every nation. Both the United States and the Soviet Union stockpiled arsenals of conventional weapons and thermonuclear warheads, and rising political and military tensions between the two nations threatened stability and peace across the globe.

By the start of the 1950s, U.S. political leaders had begun to believe in the "domino theory." They believed that when one country came under the control of Communists, neighboring countries were likely to follow, just like a row of dominoes falls after the first one is nudged. President Lyndon B. Johnson cited this theory in 1965 when he told the American people why he thought the country needed to join the fight in Vietnam: "If this little nation goes down the drain and can't maintain her independence, ask yourself, what is going to happen to all the other little nations?" he said. "So somebody must stand there and try to help the little nations protect themselves from the nations who would provoke aggression."[1]

Fighting for Control

In Vietnam, the governments in the North and South fought for dominance.

Each was helped by other countries that wanted to take advantage of Vietnam's strategic position on the globe. In the North, a Communist government was in control, aided by the Soviets and the Chinese, who supplied weapons, money, and military advisors. They wanted to ensure North Vietnam remained Communist. In the South, a weak, corrupt government was held in place with the support of American money and diplomacy. The United States and a few of its allies provided weapons, money, and troops to the South. Townsend Hoopes, a former undersecretary of the U.S. Air Force and the author of several books and essays on Vietnam, explained the reason for American involvement in Southeast Asia:

> *Every American policy in Vietnam ... ranging from economic aid to military training to military supply to sending of advisors, continued to be based on what seemed a self-evident proposition: namely, that the expansion of "International Communism" presented everywhere, and in nearly every form, a direct menace to U.S. security that had to be stopped—in the last resort by whatever means necessary.*[2]

In an effort to stop Vietnamese Communists from taking control, American political leaders sent thousands of military advisors to the country to train and guide the South Vietnamese army. Eventually, the United States committed hundreds of thousands of its own troops as well as billions of dollars in military aid. However, despite being the wealthiest country in the world, the United States was unable to achieve its aims in Vietnam. The war ended in a humiliating defeat for the superpower.

Today, almost 50 years after the war ended, Vietnam remains a Communist regime. However, the rest of the world has changed dramatically. The Soviet Union collapsed in 1991. China is a major force in the world's economy, but international Communism is no longer considered a threat to democracy. During the long years of the Vietnam War, few—if any—would have imagined these outcomes.

CHAPTER ONE

THE SEARCH FOR INDEPENDENCE

Trung Trac and Trung Nhi were sisters and rebel leaders in ancient Vietnam. Legend holds that these two first-century heroines killed a tiger and wrote out their demands for the Vietnamese people on its skin. They led an army of 80,000 to drive Chinese invaders out of their homeland. Three dozen of their army were highly trained women who the Trung sisters made generals. A 15th-century poem states, "All the male heroes bowed their heads in submission; Only the two sisters proudly stood up to avenge the country."[3] Although the sisters were eventually defeated, they remain legendary figures in Vietnamese history. The Trung sisters were among the first to fight for Vietnam's independence, but they were far from the last.

Nearly 2,000 years later, the Vietnamese people were once again led against invaders by a revolutionary figure. This time, it was the charismatic and fierce nationalist Nguyen Tat Thanh, better known as Ho Chi Minh, or "he who enlightens."

From China to France

Vietnam stretches over 127,000 square miles (329,000 sq km). It borders the South China Sea in a region known as Indochina. The Chinese ruled Vietnam for much of its history, although there were brief moments of independence. Even during those periods, however, life was not peaceful. Civil wars were common. Emperors were ineffective. Often, the real power was restricted to powerful clans and wealthy families.

After French Catholic missionaries arrived in Vietnam during the 1830s, they were quickly followed by French soldiers. During this period, European colonial rule was spreading throughout Africa and Asia. Great Britain, France,

Germany, Belgium, and other nations sent armies to open trade routes and stake claims to natural resources found on these large continents.

On August 31, 1858, an armada of 14 warships sailed into the port city of Da Nang in Vietnam and unloaded more than 2,000 French soldiers. They were not prepared for the resistance they faced from the Vietnamese, but that was not the extent of their troubles. They were also ill-equipped to deal with Vietnam's hot, wet climate. Hundreds died in guerrilla attacks, but many also died from disease. France only gained control when a second invasion force arrived in 1859 and seized the city of Saigon in southern Vietnam. Vietnam was officially declared a French colony. Soon, France took over the neighboring countries of Laos and Cambodia, too.

Lenin's Influence and Liberation

For decades, the French stayed in power even amid the demands of defending their native soil during World War I, which lasted from 1914 to 1918. When the war ended, the Allies (France, Great Britain, the United States, and others that had been on the same side during the war) met in Paris to negotiate the Treaty of Versailles. Ho Chi Minh was living in France at this time, acting as leader to the Vietnamese people living there. During the negotiations, Ho asked for admission to the peace conference to speak on behalf of Vietnamese independence. He was denied, and France remained in control of Vietnam.

Shortly after the peace conference, Ho helped found the French Communist Party. He had studied the writings of the Bolshevik leader Vladimir Lenin. (The Bolsheviks were radicals in the Russian Social-Democratic Workers' Party who formed the Communist Party in 1918 in Russia.) Lenin had called for resistance from people of the world whose countries had been colonized by European powers. "What emotion, enthusiasm and clear-sightedness, and confidence [Lenin] instilled in me!" Ho recalled years later. "Though sitting alone in my room, I shouted aloud as if addressing large crowds: 'Dear martyrs, compatriots! This is what we need, this is what we need, this is the path to our liberation.'"[4]

In 1940, shortly after the onset of World War II, Nazi Germany conquered France, and thus gained control over Vietnam. Germany turned Vietnam over to Japan, its ally in Asia. Ho returned to Southeast Asia and formed the Viet Minh, a group that aimed to unify Vietnam under one government. Ho organized the group while he and his followers hid from the Japanese in a cave near the village of Pac Bo.

Ho had grand plans for his country's future. "The hour has struck!" Ho declared in the Viet Minh's first message to the Vietnamese people. "Raise aloft the insurrectionary banner and guide the people throughout the country to overthrow the Japanese and the French!

The sacred call of the Fatherland is resounding in your ears; the blood of our heroic predecessors who sacrificed their lives is stirring in your hearts! … Let us rise up quickly! … Victory to Viet-Nam's Revolution!"[5]

Ho Chi Minh, shown here in 1946, was a revolutionary who sought to unify the Vietnamese people and achieve independence for his country.

THE HO CHI MINH TRAIL

The Ho Chi Minh Trail was established to equip Communist guerrillas in South Vietnam with arms, ammunition, and other supplies. The trail was not a single passageway but a network of dirt roads and paths well hidden in the jungle. The trail twisted down from North Vietnam, through parts of Laos and Cambodia, into South Vietnam. To the North Vietnamese, the trail was known as the Truong Son Road, named for the chain of mountains that it passed through.

The trail was opened in 1959 by a North Vietnamese army engineering unit, but was little used until the 1960s, when it was expanded. Soon, dozens of trucks carrying supplies were being driven down the trail each week. They were guided by guerrillas who knew every turn and hazard along its thousands of miles. Over the years, the North Vietnamese and Communist guerrillas known as the Viet Cong improved the route, widening the roads and paving its entire length.

The Ho Chi Minh Trail was an important route for North Vietnamese soldiers transporting supplies.

With the Help of "Uncle Ho"

The Viet Minh soon became a popular force among the Vietnamese. The country's years under French and Japanese rule had been brutal. During World War II, more than 2 million Vietnamese died from starvation as the Japanese and French gave available food to their troops, and the Japanese shipped food back to Japan to relieve hunger problems there. In response, Ho's Viet Minh guerrillas urged peasants to raid food warehouses and distribute the rice and grain. To the Vietnamese, Ho became known as "Uncle Ho." They saw him as a kind and generous person who would lead them to better lives.

Armed mostly with spears and machetes, the Viet Minh guerrillas fought the Japanese. Eventually, the United States sent commandos into Vietnam to better arm and train the Viet Minh guerrillas in their war against the Japanese. In return, Ho provided his new allies with intelligence on Japanese troop movements. The Americans prepared the Vietnamese to attack Japanese strongholds. Realizing their position was too vulnerable, the Japanese soon withdrew from the country.

Ho had a plan for his country. First, he wanted total independence. Second, he wanted to completely reorganize the nation's economy. He planned to seize land and property from rich landowners who had worked with the French and return it to the peasants. This plan did not happen. China and Great Britain had different ideas. China sent troops into North Vietnam. Britain and France put troops in South Vietnam and armed them so they could fight the Viet Minh. Once again, Ho pleaded for independence. He sent his request to America's new president, Harry S. Truman, and once again, he was ignored.

In August 1945, just days after the United States dropped atomic bombs on Japan, Ho and the Viet Minh marched into Vietnam's capital of Hanoi. They declared themselves the rightful rulers of the country. Ho called this event the August Revolution. A few weeks later, on September 2, 1945, 400,000 Vietnamese citizens gathered in Ba Dinh Square in Hanoi to hear Ho declare the day to be Vietnam's Independence Day. He spoke to the people as the self-proclaimed leader of a new country—the Democratic Republic of Vietnam.

Ho Chi Minh was seen as "Uncle Ho," a man who loved the Vietnamese people and looked out for their best interests.

At Odds with France

Ho's nationalist government did not last long. Soon, more than 200,000 Chinese troops moved into the North and took control. By 1946, Ho had begun talking with the French government. Although he did not want the French in charge, he reluctantly agreed that Vietnam would belong to France, as long as France considered Vietnam a free state within the French Union and would grant Vietnam the right to elect its own government. China, unwilling to go to war with France, then withdrew its troops from Vietnam. In May, Ho went to Paris, France, planning to negotiate the details of Vietnam's election process and its role as an independent republic.

However, Ho and Vietnamese negotiators soon realized the French had never actually intended to withdraw from Vietnam. Only North Vietnam was going to be free. French leaders regarded South Vietnam as a separate country, often referred to as Cochinchina. They planned to retain control there.

Negotiations dragged on throughout the summer of 1946. Ho insisted that the South and North be unified, but the French refused. Vietnamese negotiator Pham Van Dong later recalled the contempt from the French. "When the meeting began," according to Pham, "the chief of the French delegation, Max Andre, said to me, 'We only need an ordinary police operation for eight days to clean all of you out.' There was no need for negotiations."[6]

When Ho returned to Hanoi in the fall of 1946, there was still no agreement with the French—and tensions were rising. In Ho's absence, sporadic fighting had broken out between Viet Minh guerrillas and French troops. In November, the French shelled the harbor city of Haiphong, a major hub of Viet Minh resistance. Around 6,000 Vietnamese died in the attack. The French next turned their attention to Hanoi. They drove the Viet Minh, including Ho, into the mountains surrounding the city. On December 19, believing he had no other choice, Ho declared war on France.

An Ongoing Battle

As the First Indochina War began, the French had a definite military advantage. The Viet Minh were poorly armed. The French had modern weapons, mostly supplied by the United States, which feared a Communist takeover of Vietnam. However, the Viet Minh guerrillas had widespread support among the peasants. In an interview with PBS, Nguyen Thi Dinh said,

At first we did not have any weapons except for bamboo spears. But in the northern part of our country, they were producing arms. I was appointed to go there to report on the situation in the South. Uncle Ho told me that he carried the South in the depth of his heart, and I should tell him what we needed so that the central government could supply us to fight the French and drive them out of the country. I replied that we needed guns. Uncle Ho said that the central government could only give us so many guns because they did not have many. The main thing, he said, was to capture the enemy's guns and use these guns against them.[7]

As the Viet Minh struggled, French leaders took charge in Hanoi, where in 1949, they installed a puppet government led by Bao Dai, a former Vietnamese emperor.

Around this time, major changes were happening in China. The country's Communist and Nationalist forces started a civil war, and the Nationalists were driven out of mainland China to the island of Taiwan, leaving Communists in power of the world's most populous country. This government, led by Mao Zedong, started supplying the Viet Minh with guns and military advisors, making the group a much more formidable opponent. In addition, Mao extended diplomatic recognition to Ho's government. This made China the first foreign power to recognize Ho Chi Minh as Vietnam's leader. The Soviet Union soon extended diplomatic recognition to Ho as well. The United States had been helping pay for France's war against the Viet Minh. Now, it believed it

had no alternative but to recognize Bao Dai's regime as the legitimate government of Vietnam.

Communist battles raged in other countries, as well. In 1950, North Korean Communist troops aided by China invaded South Korea. Fearing that China planned to spread Communism throughout Asia, the United States mobilized an international military force to repel the attack.

Meanwhile, the United States also stepped up its financial assistance for the French effort against the Communists in Vietnam. Despite this substantial aid, the French scored few military

Mao Zedong, the chairman of the Communist Party of China, helped strengthen the Viet Minh.

successes. The French would capture and occupy a rural village or an urban area, only to see guerrillas take it back within a matter of weeks. In May 1954, the most influential battle of the First Indochina War occurred. At Dien Bien Phu in northwestern Vietnam, a Viet Minh force crushed the French army.

A Conference in Geneva

On May 8, a day after the fall of Dien Bien Phu, representatives from Vietnam, the United States, China, France, the Soviet Union, Laos, and Cambodia met in Geneva, Switzerland, for the continuation of a peace conference that had started in April. Vietnam was granted its independence along with Laos and Cambodia. However, the compromise agreement called for Vietnam to be divided along the 17th parallel of latitude, temporarily creating two independent countries. The North would be turned over to Ho's Communists. The South would be controlled by Bao Dai. National elections, with the goal of reuniting the country, were scheduled for 1956. The Soviets and Chinese urged Ho to accept the deal. They feared the United States would intervene with troops if Ho attempted to take control of the entire country.

Ho grudgingly accepted the terms. He was confident that he enjoyed the support of the Vietnamese people and that the Communists would win the 1956 unification election. Ho returned to Hanoi, where he took power as head of the Democratic Republic of Vietnam,

or North Vietnam. In the South, Bao Dai appointed the strongly anti-communist politician Ngo Dinh Diem as the country's prime minister.

Under President Dwight D. Eisenhower, the United States continued to support global anticommunist movements. Beginning in 1954, America sent $100 million a year in aid to Diem's government in Saigon. In 1955, Diem held a referendum on the future of Bao Dai's monarchy, rigging the vote to get the result he wanted. Three days later, he declared himself the president of South Vietnam. That year, the first American military advisors arrived in Saigon to help train the South Vietnamese army. With the Americans propping up the South Vietnamese government and the Soviets and Chinese helping Ho in the North, unification hardly seemed possible.

Moats and Fences

When Ngo Dinh Diem declared that the South would not participate in national elections, guerrilla warfare erupted between the North and the South. Communists infiltrated Saigon. They assassinated government officials and ambushed soldiers and police. In 1959, a secret supply line—the Ho Chi Minh Trail—was cut through the jungle. It linked the North and the South, but also snaked through Cambodia and Laos. It was used to ship arms to Communist guerrillas in the South. A year later, an independent organization of Communist guerrillas formed the National

TRENCHES, TUNNELS, AND CANNONS

During the siege at Dien Bien Phu, Viet Minh soldiers dug miles of trenches and tunnels around the French positions, creating a network of hiding places from which they could launch assaults on the enemy. In *Vietnam: A History*, Stanley Karnow quoted Viet Minh colonel Bui Tin: "The shovel became our most important weapon. Everyone dug tunnels and trenches under fire, sometimes hitting hard soil and only advancing five or six yards a day. But we gradually surrounded Dien Bien Phu with an underground network several hundred miles long, and we could tighten the noose around the French."[1]

Meanwhile, the Viet Minh hauled heavy cannons high into the mountains—a feat French military leaders had thought impossible. Karnow quoted one French officer, Colonel Charles Piroth, who boasted, "No Viet Minh cannon will be able to fire three rounds before being destroyed by my artillery."[2] Nevertheless, with artillery shells raining down from above and guerrillas attacking from secret hiding places in the valley, it took only 55 days for the nearly 16,000 French paratroopers trapped at Dien Bien Phu to succumb to the onslaught.

Using miles of tunnels such as this one, the Viet Minh surrounded and conquered French troops occupying Dien Bien Phu.

1. Quoted in Stanley Karnow, *Vietnam: A History*. New York, NY: Penguin, 1983, p. 196.
2. Quoted in Karnow, *Vietnam: A History*, p. 195.

Liberation Front. Known more familiarly as the Viet Cong, it became a close ally of the North in the years ahead.

Diem's regime was plagued by corruption. Diem's brother Ngo Dinh Nhu, head of the secret police, used repressive and cold-blooded tactics to find Communist rebels. Nhu's secret police searched rural villages, taking young men suspected of guerrilla activity away from their families. The police often tortured or murdered suspected members of the Viet Cong. The Viet Cong guerrillas fought back. In addition to assassinating South Vietnamese officials, they won peasants over by promising them their own land and pledging to put an end to Diem's and Nhu's abuse.

In response, Diem ordered the construction of thousands of fortified villages, known as strategic hamlets. Each was surrounded by moats and barbed-wire fences. Tens of thousands of peasants were herded into these villages to keep them isolated from the Viet Cong. Even so, the Viet Cong soon found ways to break in.

A Horrifying Protest

By 1963, it was clear that Ngo Dinh Diem's regime was teetering on the edge of chaos. On May 8, an incident occurred in the city of Hue that led to his downfall. It also made it extremely clear to U.S. diplomats that unless they stepped in and stabilized the shaky government in the South, it would fall to the Communists.

On that day, a group of Buddhist monks had gathered in Hue to celebrate a religious holiday. A low-level city official sent in police to break up the gathering. Word quickly spread through the Buddhist community. Within hours, several thousand Buddhists gathered in front of a radio station to listen to a speech broadcast by one of their leaders. When police arrived at the radio station, they fired into the crowd, killing nine people.

Outraged, Buddhist leaders organized demonstrations throughout the country. Ngo Dinh Diem, a Catholic, shrugged off the protests. He claimed they were staged by the Communists. However, instead of backing down, the Buddhists stepped up their protests and called for an end to his rule. Many demonstrators were confronted by Ngo Dinh Nhu's agents, who roughed them up or hauled them away to jail.

On the morning of June 11, an elderly Buddhist monk sat down cross-legged in the middle of a busy Saigon intersection. As a form of protest, another monk covered him with gasoline and then set the man on fire. News photographers captured the image of the burning Buddhist monk. The next day, the horrifying pictures were published on the front pages of newspapers all over the world, and the photo became one of the most powerful and iconic images to come out of the Vietnam War.

Soon, other Buddhists carried out similar demonstrations. They vowed the burnings would continue until

Photographs such as this one of a Buddhist monk sacrificing his life in protest were seen around the world.

Ngo Dinh Diem granted them religious freedom. Convinced that Communists had encouraged the suicides to destabilize his regime, he refused to yield.

An End to Diem

Ngo Dinh Diem was right to worry about his role. His top military leaders no longer wanted him in power. U.S. officials also wanted him out. By that point, the United States was spending more than $1 million a day to prop up Diem's government and provide guidance to the South Vietnamese army. Additionally, there were more than 16,000 American military advisors still stationed in South Vietnam.

Finally, a group of South Vietnamese generals approached a U.S. Central Intelligence Agency (CIA) official, Lucien Conein, and asked for U.S. support in toppling Diem. Their request was forwarded to President John F. Kennedy.

South Vietnamese leader Ngo Dinh Diem faced opposition at home and from abroad.

FIRST LADY OF VIETNAM

The wife of South Vietnamese secret police leader Ngo Dinh Nhu—and Diem's sister-in-law—was known to the world as Madame Nhu. Since Diem was not married, Madame Nhu served as the first lady of Vietnam during his regime, from 1955 until 1963.

Born Tran Le Xuan in 1924, Madame Nhu had a taste for Western fashion and style and a fiery attitude. She often publicly made fun of enemies of the Diem regime. In 1963, when the first Buddhist monk burned himself to death, Madame Nhu told an American television reporter, "What have the Buddhist leaders done comparatively ... The only thing they have done, they have barbecued one of their monks whom they have intoxicated ... and even that barbecuing was done not even with self-sufficient means because they used imported gasoline."[1]

When Madame Nhu visited America in November 1963, South Vietnamese leaders staged a coup against Diem, murdering him along with Madame Nhu's husband. The new regime barred her from returning to Vietnam. She lived in Europe until her death on April 24, 2011, at the age of 86.

Madame Nhu was known not only for her fashion sense, but also for her sarcasm and strong opinions.

1. Quoted in American Experience, "Vietnam Online," PBS, accessed on September 6, 2018. www.shoppbs.pbs.org/wgbh/amex/vietnam/series/pt_02.html.

He decided that Diem should be given the opportunity to resign. In Saigon, U.S. ambassador Henry Cabot Lodge Jr. communicated the ultimatum to Diem. The Vietnamese president refused to step down.

South Vietnamese military leaders now felt justified in resorting to force. On November 1, planes bombed the presidential residence in Saigon. Army troops searched the city for Diem and Nhu, who were found hiding in a Catholic church. They were arrested and quickly executed.

A New Battle Begins

After the collapse of Diem's regime, South Vietnam continued to struggle. It was governed by a shaky military regime unable to stabilize the nation. Seeing this weakness, the Viet Cong grew bolder. In the countryside and in city streets, they stepped up attacks and assassinations of government officials—all with the support of Ho's government.

In August 1964, three North Vietnamese gunboats patrolling the Gulf of Tonkin were alleged to have fired on a U.S. Navy destroyer, the *Maddox*. Two days later the *Maddox* and another destroyer, the *Turner Joy*, reported that they were under a renewed attack. President Lyndon B. Johnson, who had taken office after the assassination of President John F. Kennedy in November 1963, heard about the attack. Johnson and his advisors were

Aggression against the United States from North Vietnamese ships in the Gulf of Tonkin caused an increase in hostilities.

not certain about exactly what had happened. (Weeks later Johnson admitted to his secretary of defense he doubted the second attack had actually occurred.) Nonetheless, they used the event as an opportunity to commit to a full military response against Vietnam's Communist threat. At Johnson's urging, on August 7, 1964, the U.S. Congress passed the Gulf of Tonkin Resolution. It granted Johnson power to use force in Southeast Asia. Although the resolution fell short of an actual declaration of war, Johnson used its authority to justify sending American troops to fight for South Vietnam. American involvement in the Second Indochina War—known to Americans as the Vietnam War—had begun.

After President Lyndon B. Johnson signed the Gulf of Tonkin Resolution in 1964, the United States became heavily involved in the Vietnam War.

CHAPTER TWO

SPREADING AND EXPANDING

The United States was determined to subdue the North Vietnamese. During the spring of 1965, they bombed key targets in North Vietnam and sent in thousands of ground troops. Faced with such military might, the United States believed Ho Chi Minh would finally ask for peace.

However, Ho did not surrender. The Communists in the North kept fighting, relying heavily on the Soviet Union and China for supplies and arms, and American soldiers found themselves fighting an enemy that was difficult to find. They went from village to village in search of guerrilla fighters, struggling to catch them. The North Vietnamese were skilled at striking quickly and then melting back into the thick jungle. By 1969, 530,000 American troops were in South Vietnam, but sheer numbers were not enough to claim victory. No matter what strategy they tried, they always seemed a step behind.

Attacking Americans

The first battle began moments before dawn on November 1, 1964 when 100 Viet Cong guerrillas hiding in the jungle fired mortars and cannons at an American air base at Bien Hoa, north of Saigon. The American and South Vietnamese soldiers were caught completely unaware, and the guerrillas had disappeared before the soldiers could get organized for a counterattack. As daylight appeared, the Americans assessed the damage. Four Americans and two South Vietnamese had been killed. More than 70 soldiers were wounded. Seven planes had been destroyed and 16 more damaged.

More attacks followed, and not only on military bases. On December 24, 1964, a group of American officers were gathered in the bar of the Brinks Hotel in downtown Saigon for a Christmas Eve party. Suddenly, a bomb exploded. Two Americans were killed and

The military base of Pleiku, shown here, was located in Vietnam's Central Highlands. It was the site of a surprise attack by the Viet Cong in 1965.

65 injured. Two Viet Cong guerrillas had set off the bomb. They had been tipped off by a spy who had infiltrated the South Vietnamese government and knew where the Americans would be.

The Viet Cong staged another attack before dawn on February 7, 1965. They targeted an American army base at Pleiku, nearly 300 miles (483 km) north of Saigon in a mountainous region known as the Central Highlands. The Viet Cong found the Americans sleeping and hurled shells into the camp from their jungle hideouts. This time, eight Americans were killed, while another hundred suffered wounds. By staging such daring attacks, the Viet Cong showed the Americans they would challenge them anywhere.

To combat guerrillas attacking from the jungle, soldiers planted explosives in hideaways and tunnels.

Getting in Deeper

As U.S. troops were heading to Vietnam, American leaders sought a peaceful end to the conflict. President Johnson sent a message to the North Vietnamese: The United States would fund a massive public works project to develop dams and hydroelectric plants along the Mekong River. The project could be an economic boost that would benefit a huge region of Southeast Asia. However, in exchange, the Communists would have to give up their claim to South Vietnam. After making the offer, Johnson boasted to an aide, "Old Ho can't turn that down."[8]

Again, the United States had misjudged Ho. He rejected the deal, and the attacks on U.S. troops continued. At last, Johnson resolved to get tough with the Communists. "I've gone far enough," Johnson said to his aides. "I've had enough of this."[9] He launched Operation Rolling Thunder, a series of bombing missions attacking military targets in the North. The missions also targeted the Ho Chi Minh Trail in an effort to wipe out Ho's supply line to

U.S. Air Force bombers played a major role during Operation Rolling Thunder.

the South. The first bombs fell on North Vietnamese targets on March 2, 1965.

Under the plan for Operation Rolling Thunder, the military would not  attack civilian targets. For example, the huge dikes holding the Red River back from heavily populated sections of the North were off limits. If the dikes had burst, they would have released billions of gallons of water. The resulting floods might have killed hundreds of thousands of North Vietnamese peasants. The catastrophe would certainly have thrown the Communist government into chaos, but Johnson had decided early in the war to spare civilians. Still, the bombing was relentless. Even though civilians were not specifically targeted, many—such as those working in or around factories or facilities that were targeted—died in the aerial attacks.

Some officials in Washington were unsure that the bombing campaign was actually hurting the North Vietnamese. They pointed out that there were few war-related industries in the North. Instead, most of their weapons and military supplies came from the Soviets and Chinese. Undersecretary of State George Ball explained his perspective:

> I was convinced that we were not going to achieve our will by bombing the North; that in the first place, it was a fairly primitive industrial society, and that there weren't the kind of targets that were adapted for strategic bombing. And secondly, I was convinced that we would never break the will of a determined people by simply bombing; and in fact, we would probably tend to unite them more than ever.[10]

"BURY ME WITH SOLDIERS"

In 1969, 22-year-old Private Charles Fink had been in Vietnam for only a few weeks when he was leading the 199th Infantry Brigade through thick jungle vegetation east of Saigon. Suddenly, a mine exploded. Almost all of Fink's patrol died. He wrote a poem in tribute to his lost friends and the bonds they had shared. The poem is now read at many Vietnam War veterans' funerals. In part, it reads:

> It's funny when you think of it,
> The way we got along.
> We'd come from different worlds
> To live in one no one belongs.
> I didn't even like them all and,
> I'm sure they'd all agree.
> Yet, I would give my life for them,
> I hope. Some did for me.
> So bury me with soldiers, please
> Though much maligned they be,
> Yes, bury me with soldiers, for
> I miss their company.[1]

1. Quoted in Martha Evans, "Charles Fink's 'Bury Me with Soldiers' Poem about Vietnam Endures," *Long Island Newsday*, August 5, 2018. www.newsday.com/long-island/vietnam-war-poem-priest-long-island-funerals-1.20240871.

In addition, the Americans could not easily cut off the supply of war materials from the North to the South. The network of paths and roads making up the Ho Chi Minh Trail was well hidden by the heavy jungle foliage. It was virtually impossible to spot from the air. Each week, dozens of North Vietnamese trucks rolled along the trail, bringing arms, ammunition, and other supplies to the Viet Cong insurgents in the South.

Swelling Ranks of Soldiers

The first American ground troops arrived in Vietnam on March 8, 1965. More than 3,000 marines landed at Da Nang to protect an air base located near the coastal city. By the end of the year, 200,000 American troops were stationed in South Vietnam.

Troops also came from a handful of American allies, including South Korea, Thailand, Australia, New Zealand, and the Philippines. Leaders of these Pacific

Rim countries believed too much Chinese or Soviet influence in Southeast Asia could harm them.

However, South Vietnam and the United States supplied most of the manpower for the war. To provide troops, the U.S. Congress reinstituted the draft, which forced young men into military service—an action that proved to be very unpopular with Americans. Draft resistance began as soon as the first young men were called to military service. By the middle of 1965, 380 American men had been arrested for refusing to join the military.

With the addition of the draftees, the American military had enough troops to wage a full-scale invasion of North Vietnam. However, in late 1965, Chinese leaders warned Johnson that if the American military crossed the 17th parallel, China would send its army

Anti-war protests often included young men burning their draft cards.

to defend North Vietnam. This would turn the conflict into a full-scale war between two major powers. Johnson thought it best to heed China's warning. He told his commanders not to invade. Instead, America focused on bombing military targets in the North and rooting out Communist guerrillas in the South.

American troops were sent into rural villages to search for evidence of Viet Cong involvement. Suspected guerrillas were taken into custody. Any hut found with hidden weapons or ammunition was burned. At first, this strategy was successful. The Viet Cong fled deeper into the jungle. However, American military leaders failed to realize that these attacks only caused more peasants to join the enemy.

In 1965, CBS News reporter Morley Safer reported on one such operation in the village of Cam Se:

The day's operation burned down 150 houses, wounded three women, killed one baby, wounded one Marine and netted four prisoners. Four old men who could not answer questions put to them in English. Four old men who had no idea what an I.D. card was. Today's operation is the frustration of Vietnam in miniature. There is little doubt that American firepower can win a military victory here. But to a Vietnamese peasant … it will take more than presidential promises to convince him that we are on his side.[11]

The Americans had to carry the brunt of the fighting because the South Vietnamese army, known as the Army of the Republic of Vietnam (ARVN), was simply not effective. The Viet Cong soon realized this as well. For years, the Viet Cong had conducted a loosely structured guerrilla campaign, but in 1965, the guerrillas started forming into regiments and attacking the South Vietnamese in direct combat. In May 1965, Viet Cong regiments overran South Vietnamese units in Song Be, around 50 miles (80 km) from Saigon, and in Quang Ngai, a city along the coast. The ARVN's worst defeat was suffered at the town of Dong Xoai, where more than 800 South Vietnamese soldiers were killed in a Viet Cong raid.

Escalations

For the next two years, U.S. ground troops fought guerrillas in the South as American bombers attacked targets in the North. While President Johnson occasionally ordered halts to the air war in hopes of luring the North Vietnamese to the bargaining table, these overtures all failed. U.S. soldiers continued to pour into South Vietnam. By early 1967, more than 360,000 had arrived.

South Vietnam was going through changes and finally had a stable government. After Diem, various military commanders had taken a turn at controlling the government. Most of them were corrupt and unpopular with the people. Then, in 1967, the South Vietnamese

Marines, such as those shown here, were the first U.S. troops to officially fight on the ground in Vietnam in 1965.

THE FIGHT FROM ABOVE

Just as World War II was marked by the heavy use of fighter planes, the Vietnam War was marked by the heavy use of helicopters. According to a 2018 report from the Vietnam Helicopter Pilots Association, about 12,000 helicopters were put into service during the Vietnam War. About half of these were shot down and destroyed. More than 2,000 pilots died, and more than 2,700 other personnel were also killed.

At one point, the American company Bell Aerospace proposed another technology: soldiers with jetpacks. Bell wanted to create a variety of jetpacks to be used for surveillance and launching assaults. Those plans never got off the ground, however. It quickly became clear that soldiers using jetpacks would be far too vulnerable to enemy fire.

Some helicopters were equipped with loudspeakers so that messages could be broadcast to the Vietnamese in areas controlled by the Viet Cong.

elected as president Nguyen Van Thieu, a career military officer and Viet Minh member. During his presidency, Thieu's administration faced accusations of corruption. However, his government survived with the popular support of the South Vietnamese.

Near the end of 1967, the American commander in Vietnam, General William Westmoreland, delivered a rosy prediction about the progress of the war. He suggested the tide had turned in favor of the Americans and South Vietnamese. On a visit to Washington, D.C., in November 1967, Westmoreland told journalists that the United States had contained the Viet Cong guerrillas and slowed the shipment of arms and supplies to the Viet Cong in the South. The bombing campaign in the North had worn down the will of the Communists to fight. "It is significant that the enemy has not won a major battle in more than a year," Westmoreland boasted. "In general, he can fight his large forces only at the edges of his sanctuaries … His guerrilla force is declining at a steady rate."[12]

Other officials echoed those remarks. During a visit to Saigon, Vice President Hubert Humphrey told reporters, "We are beginning to win this struggle. We are on the offensive. Territory is being gained. We are making steady progress."[13] However, these words were premature. Events that unfolded in the next few weeks proved Humphrey, Westmoreland, and the other supporters of the war effort terribly wrong.

U.S. president Lyndon B. Johnson (left) is shown here during a visit to South Vietnam in 1966, with General William Westmoreland, Lieutenant General Nguyen Van Thieu, and Prime Minister Nguyen Cao Ky.

Khe Sanh

Even as Westmoreland told reporters that the end of the war was in sight, his subordinates in South Vietnam were monitoring massive troop movements in the North. This indicated that the North was planning a major offensive. It came on January 21, 1968, when the Communists struck a U.S. Marine Corps air base at Khe Sanh, just south of the 17th parallel. The attack was significant because it was waged not by Viet Cong guerrillas but by a force of 20,000 soldiers from the North Vietnamese army. That marked the first time in the war that the North had directly confronted American troops.

Even with only 6,000 marines to hold the base, the American soldiers withstood the attack, supported by a bombing campaign that pushed the North Vietnamese army away from the air base.

The siege of Khe Sanh was not an isolated attack. For months, the Communists had been planning a major assault on South Vietnam in an effort to gain the upper hand. The prime thrust of the siege would be the major cities of the South, including Saigon. Viet Cong guerrillas intended to confront defenders head-on and, they hoped, stir up passions among the South Vietnamese for liberation. North Vietnamese leaders believed that the Americans were unpopular in the South. They hoped that once southern city dwellers saw an offensive waged against the Americans, these citizens would join their fight.

Khe Sanh was actually planned as a distraction. North Vietnamese military leaders hoped the United States would rush troops north to defend the base. This would leave Saigon and the other targeted cities with fewer defenders. The U.S. military did not react as the North Vietnamese had calculated, however. Instead, the Americans used air power to end the siege at Khe Sanh. Despite this response, the North Vietnamese proceeded with their original plan. On January 31, the North Vietnamese army and Viet Cong launched a series of coordinated attacks. They chose their moment carefully. The attacks came during Tet, a major Vietnamese holiday celebrating the beginning of the Lunar New Year.

A Devastated City

Up until then, both the Northern and Southern armies had respected Tet with a cease-fire. However, with the latest attacks, the North Vietnamese generals decided to seize the element of surprise. They knew that many South Vietnamese soldiers would be home for the holiday, celebrating with their families. The attacks, which became known as the Tet Offensive, stretched on for five months. Approximately 60 cities and smaller communities in the South were targeted, although the major fighting was concentrated in Saigon and the city of Hue, north of Da Nang.

One of Vietnam's most historic cities, Hue was at one time the capital of the Nguyen dynasty, which had ruled

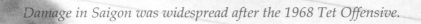
Damage in Saigon was widespread after the 1968 Tet Offensive.

Vietnam from the 17th to 19th centuries. Hue features many pagoda-style buildings, including the sprawling palace known as the Citadel, and was regarded as the most cosmopolitan city in Vietnam, thanks to its gourmet restaurants, ornate palaces, and striking outdoor statuary.

The North Vietnamese army and Viet Cong guerrillas met little resistance in Hue at first, overrunning the city on January 31. They arrested government officials, police officers, and thousands of civilians suspected of collaborating with the Americans. Most of those arrested would receive no mercy from the Communists. In a month, as many as 3,000 civilians were murdered, their bodies thrown into shallow graves. Later, when the graves were dug up, the remains showed that many of the victims had been shot with their hands tied behind their backs.

Hoping to spare damage to Hue's many historic buildings, U.S. commanders decided not to repel the attack on the city with an air strike. Instead, they dispatched U.S. Army and U.S. Marine battalions to defend the city. The troops came under heavy fire. For the next 26 days, the Battle of Hue was fiercely fought street by street and house by house. By the time the Communist troops were driven out of the city, around 8,000 North Vietnamese and Viet Cong fighters had been killed. Besides the 3,000 civilians who had been massacred by the Communists, several thousand more were killed in the crossfire. In addition, 384 South Vietnamese and 216 American troops lost their lives.

"Throughout all of this, you constantly had this fear," said U.S. Marine

U.S. Marines are shown here during the attack on the city of Hue, which was part of the Tet Offensive.

PHOTOS FROM VIETNAM

One of the most horrific photographs from the Tet Offensive was taken on February 1, 1968, as Viet Cong guerrillas swarmed into Saigon streets. General Nguyen Ngoc Loan, the chief of the South Vietnamese national police, is seen in the photograph executing a Viet Cong guerrilla in the photo. Only minutes earlier, the guerrilla had murdered a policeman and his family. The photograph captures the moment Loan fires a pistol at his grimacing prisoner.

The photograph was published on the front pages of newspapers throughout the United States and other countries. It had a chilling effect on readers, who suddenly saw vivid evidence of the Vietnam War's brutality. In 1969, American news photographer Eddie Adams won the Pulitzer Prize for this photo.

Adams later said he had seen the guerrilla led out of a building by police officers. He hurried over and raised his camera, thinking the picture would simply be a routine photograph of a man being taken prisoner. Suddenly, Loan approached the prisoner. "I was about five feet away from him, and I see him reach for his pistol," Adams said. "I thought he was going to threaten the prisoner. So as quick as he brought his pistol up, I took a picture. But it turned out he shot him."[1]

Photojournalist Eddie Adams (shown here) became well-known for his famous photograph showing the execution of a Viet Cong guerrilla.

1. Quoted in Al Santoli, *To Bear Any Burden: The Vietnam War and Its Aftermath in the Words of Americans and Southeast Asians.* Bloomington, IN: Indiana University Press, 1999, p. 184.

Captain Myron Harrington, who fought in the battle of Hue. "You had this utter devastation all around you. You had this horrible smell. I mean you just cannot describe the smell of death especially when you're looking at it a couple of weeks along."[14]

The American goal to preserve Hue failed. The historic city was virtually leveled during the battle. Of its more than 17,000 homes, more than half were destroyed, while another 3,000 sustained serious damage. In addition, shelling damaged many of the city's pagodas and palaces, particularly the Citadel, which the North Vietnamese army had used as a base. When journalist Robert Shaplen toured the city after the fighting, he wrote, "Nothing I saw during the Korean War, or in the Vietnam War so far, has been as terrible, in terms of destruction and despair, as what I saw in Hue."[15]

A Stalemate and a Decision

The Tet Offensive was a disaster for the North Vietnamese army. Civilians in South Vietnam did not rally behind the Communist cause as North Vietnamese leaders had expected. Furthermore, the North Vietnamese army and Viet Cong sustained heavy casualties and gained no new territory. Their attacks in Saigon were particularly fruitless. At one point, Viet Cong guerrillas captured a radio station in Saigon so they could broadcast a taped message from Ho calling for the city's liberation. Moments after the guerrillas captured the station,

however, the power to the building was cut off, thwarting their plans. At the end of the siege, eight guerrillas inside the building detonated a bomb, destroying the radio station and taking their own lives.

An equally disastrous siege came at the U.S. embassy in Saigon. A group of Viet Cong guerrillas attacked it, blowing a hole in the wall of the compound and entering the grounds. They succeeded in driving the Marine guards inside, but because their commanders had been killed in the initial firefight, the remaining guerrillas did not know how to proceed. Instead of pressing the attack, they hesitated. Minutes later, American reinforcements arrived and killed them.

News of the Tet Offensive flooded into the United States. Teletype bulletins went out to the largest wire services. Television film footage was sent to the United States via planes and satellites. Pictures of tragedy and atrocities filled Americans' television screens, making the Vietnam War the country's first "television war."

Despite the heavy losses the North Vietnamese sustained during the Tet Offensive, it also proved that the resolve of the Communists had not diminished. It presented a dilemma for President Johnson, who was keenly aware of how unpopular the war was among Americans. He had to consider whether the United States should pull out of the war. As reporter Michael Mosettig wrote for PBS, "The pictures hit the American public and then the political scene in a presidential election campaign year more tellingly than the rockets and bullets at the embassy."[16]

On February 22, the trusted CBS news anchorman Walter Cronkite stated that forces in the Vietnam War had reached a stalemate—a term taken from chess to describe no possibility of winning. It was time for America to withdraw. Some historians believe that Cronkite's words convinced President Johnson that he would no longer have the support of the U.S. people to stay in this long war. It was likely also why, two months after the Tet Offensive, the president shocked the country by announcing that he would not seek reelection.

CHAPTER THREE

A TIME OF PROTEST

Two famous figures of the 1960s—boxer Muhammad Ali and actress Jane Fonda—both drew attention for their outspoken criticism of the Vietnam War. Their words and actions inspired many others across the country. The number of protesters at colleges and in Washington, D.C., was growing. People were sickened by what they saw on their television sets. Prior to the Tet Offensive, a Gallup Organization poll indicated that 24 percent of Americans opposed the war. In March 1968, after just two months of fighting, Gallup reported that opposition to the war had skyrocketed to 42 percent.

People were shocked by the numbers being reported in 1968: More than 31,000 American soldiers had been killed since the start of the war. More than 200,000 were injured. The war was costing more than $25 billion a year. As many as 40,000 young men were being drafted to serve every

month. Many Americans were fed up. The war in Vietnam was still raging, but the battle for the hearts and minds of the American people had already been lost.

A Divided Country

Protests against the war started almost immediately after the U.S. Congress passed the Gulf of Tonkin Resolution. By early 1965, anti-war activists were organizing peace demonstrations. Many of the demonstrations involved college students and other young people. They discovered they held enormous power to protest unfair conditions, influence policy, and sway emotions. After the bombing campaign against North Vietnam began, student leaders staged Vietnam "teach-ins" on campuses, where they debated war issues. Teach-ins were followed by bigger protests. On April 17, 1965, an organization calling itself Students for a Democratic Society (SDS) organized a protest in Washington, D.C. Between 15,000 and 25,000 students picketed the White House. Then, they gathered in front of the Washington Monument for a rally.

April 17 was chosen because it was the first day the U.S. Selective Service Commission (later called the Selective Service System) issued draft notices to young American men who had turned 19. On that day, 13,700 men received notices ordering them to report for duty. The following month, another 15,100 men were drafted. Nearly 2 million draftees would follow them in the coming years.

To protest, some men gathered around bonfires and publicly burned their draft cards. Many protesters who refused to be drafted were arrested and jailed. Thousands fled to Canada until the war ended. Thousands more applied for conscientious objector status. This exempted them from serving in combat due to religious convictions. Conscientious objectors still had to serve, but they were given jobs in the United States—generally as aides in Veterans Administration (VA) hospitals. Many young men also avoided the draft by maintaining their status as full-time college students, although this option was largely unavailable to poor, inner-city black Americans. (Later, in 1971, Congress revoked student deferments. Signing up for a college class was no longer enough to prevent being drafted.)

In an effort to make the draft fairer, in December 1969, the United States held the first draft lottery. In this system, draft-age men were given a number between 1 and 366 that corresponded to their birthday. These same numbers were written on pieces of paper, put into plastic eggs, and then randomly drawn. The men whose numbers matched those called were drafted into military service.

Even as U.S. political leaders insisted that the fight against Communism was important, other national figures publicly disagreed. Martin Luther King Jr., the nation's most important civil rights leader at the time, was one who announced his opposition to the war. In a speech delivered at a church in New York in 1967, King mentioned numerous reasons why the war must stop:

Somehow this madness must cease. We must stop now. I speak as a child of God and brother to the suffering poor of Vietnam. I speak for those whose land is being laid waste, whose homes are being destroyed, whose culture is being subverted. I speak for the poor of America who are paying the double price of smashed hopes at home and dealt death and corruption in Vietnam. I speak as a citizen of the world, for the world as it stands aghast at the path we have taken. I speak as an American to the leaders of my own nation. The great initiative in this war is ours. The initiative to stop it must be ours.[17]

Marches such as the one shown here were a common form of protest during the Vietnam War.

Following the Tet Offensive, even Washington had a growing number of politicians who were speaking out against America's involvement in the war, echoing the country's growing frustration and anger. After Johnson's decision to withdraw from the 1968 presidential race, some candidates seeking the White House openly questioned the war. They vowed that if they were elected, American troops would be brought home.

ENDING THE WAR

In the April 1965 demonstration in Washington, D.C., organized by the SDS, the group's leader, Paul Potter, addressed the crowd, saying,

> *I believe that the administration is serious about expanding the war in Asia. The question is whether the people here are as serious about ending it. I wonder what it means for each of us to say we want to end the war in Vietnam—whether, if we accept the full meaning of that statement and the gravity of the situation, we can simply leave the march and go back to the routines of a society that acts as if it were not in the midst of a grave crisis. Maybe we, like the president, are insulated from the consequences of our own decision to end the war. Maybe we have yet really to listen to the screams of a burning child and decide that we cannot go back to whatever it is we did before today until that war has ended.*[1]

1.   Paul Potter, "Name the System," in *Debating the 1960s: Liberal, Conservative, and Radical Perspectives*, Michael W. Flamm and David Steigerwald, eds. Lanham, MD: Rowman & Littlefield Publishers, 2008, p. 95.

Rioting in Chicago

That summer, anti-war activists used the Democratic National Convention being held in Chicago, Illinois, to air their concerns before a national audience. The thousands of demonstrators were met by the Chicago police, who were under orders from Mayor Richard Daley to end the protests. On August 25, 1968, rioting erupted in Grant Park, the headquarters for the peace movement. Television cameras caught police wading into the crowd, clubbing demonstrators and tossing tear gas canisters. Police even assaulted journalists. Abbie Hoffman, a radical leader of the anti-war movement, believed that these forceful police tactics only convinced more Americans that U.S. involvement in the Vietnam War was a mistake. He said,

> *At home, America sat down for the evening meal and turned on the TV, expecting the background sounds of political Muzak that had become the hallmark of a decided convention. Instead, they were presented with the shock*

of helmeted police gassing and clubbing young people to the ground. The country was instantaneously plugged and plunged into civil war. Parents fought with their kids, some of whom left home, grabbed a plane, and joined us in Chicago.[18]

After the drama in Grant Park, Hoffman and six others were charged with inciting the riots. They became known as the Chicago Seven. Their trial often took on a circus atmosphere as the defendants resorted to bizarre tactics and courtroom outbursts such as reading poetry aloud or singing. Five of the seven were convicted, but the charges were later overturned. The Chicago Seven proved to be another rallying point for anti-war activists.

A young protester is shown here standing up to armed police officers outside the 1968 Democratic National Convention held in Chicago, Illinois.

Massacre of Innocents

As demonstrators clashed with Chicago police, the fighting in Vietnam continued. Amid news of the bombings and jungle warfare, Americans caught another unsettling glimpse of the war when news outlets began reporting that American troops had massacred several hundred unarmed civilians.

On March 16, 1968, soldiers from the Charlie Company of the army's 20th Infantry Division had entered the South Vietnamese village of My Lai in Quang Ngai province. My Lai was thought to be so full of Communist activity that it was nicknamed "Pinkville." (The color red was associated with Communism.) Under Lieutenant William Calley, the company was under orders to root out the Viet Cong. Convinced that the village was teeming with guerrillas, Calley ordered a massacre. Everyone in the village—young and old—was slaughtered. Most members of Charlie Company participated in the massacre, although a few, horrified by Calley's orders, refused to kill the unarmed civilians.

The murders were stopped when a helicopter pilot, Hugh Thompson Jr., arrived on the scene and threatened to shoot any American soldiers who did not stop killing civilians. Thompson also called in other helicopters to help airlift the survivors to safety. In a 2004 interview, Thompson recalled returning to the base after the massacre. "They said I was screaming quite loud," he stated. "I threatened never to fly again. I didn't want to be a part of that. It wasn't war."[19]

At first, what happened in My Lai was hidden from the public. Initially, the army denied that U.S. soldiers had massacred civilians. Instead, they claimed that Charlie Company had killed 128 Viet Cong guerrillas and that 22 civilians had died in the battle. Within months of the slaughter, though, members of Charlie Company confided to other soldiers the truth of what had happened. One man who heard the stories was Ronald Ridenhour, who knew many members of Charlie Company. After much soul-searching, Ridenhour wrote a letter outlining what he had heard and mailed it to the president and other high-ranking government officials, including many prominent members of Congress. The letter stated, in part,

Exactly what did in fact occur in the village of Pinkville in March 1968 I do not know for certain, but I am convinced that it was something very black indeed. I remain irrevocably persuaded that if you and I do truly believe in the principles of justice and the equality of every man, however humble, before the law, that form the very backbone that this country is founded on, then we must press forward a widespread and public investigation of this matter with all our combined efforts.[20]

One recipient of the letter was

Arizona Representative Morris Udall. An opponent of the war, Udall circulated Ridenhour's letter among the members of the House Armed Services Committee, which oversees the military. Soon members of Congress were demanding answers from high-ranking officials in the Defense Department. Between 1969 and 1970, Calley and 13 other members of Charlie Company were charged with the murders of civilians at My Lai.

My Lai Goes Public

In the fall of 1969, the horrifying story of My Lai finally reached the public. Investigative journalist Seymour Hersh had heard stories about the massacre. He followed the story to Fort Benning, Georgia, where Calley was being held in the stockade pending trial. Calley gave Hersh an extensive interview, describing the massacre and contending that members of Charlie Company had simply been following orders when they wiped out the village.

In November 1969, Hersh's story about the My Lai massacre was published in newspapers throughout the country. *TIME* and *Newsweek* both put photographs of the dead civilians on their covers. The images had been captured by a military photographer, but until that point, their release had been suppressed by army officials.

When Americans saw photos from the destruction at My Lai, massive outrage erupted across the nation.

Calley and the other soldiers went on trial in 1971. After lengthy proceedings, a military court-martial convicted Calley but acquitted the other members of Charlie Company. Calley was sentenced to life in prison, but three days after the verdict was announced, President Richard M. Nixon freed the lieutenant pending his appeal. Nixon reacted to an overwhelming measure of support for Calley from the American public, who believed the lieutenant had been made a scapegoat for the murders at My Lai. Calley spent the next three years under house arrest at Fort Benning. When Calley's appeals ran out, Nixon granted him an immediate parole. Calley left the army and returned home to Georgia.

Critics of the war claimed that what happened at My Lai had almost been inevitable. Since American servicemen joined the war, they stated, they had been exposed to the most horrific forms of killing. Many of them were not prepared psychologically for what they would witness. In addition, many young men, such as Calley, were thrust into positions of leadership for which they had absolutely no training. Retired colonel George Walton of the U.S. Army remarked, "When an army is required to fight a war without the support of society it is forced to commission its Calleys."[21]

DO THE RIGHT THING

During Calley's trial, helicopter pilot Hugh Thompson Jr. testified about what he had witnessed at My Lai. After the trial ended, he returned to combat. When he finally came back to the United States, not everyone saw him as a hero. He received death threats on the phone and found dead animals laid on his porch. He told the CBS news program *60 Minutes* that he was not viewed as a good person.

In March 1998, the army presented Thompson with the Soldier's Medal, given for heroism not involving enemy conflict. Two soldiers who were with Thompson and had helped in the villagers' rescue also received the medal. The three men were honored for landing "in the line of fire between American ground troops and fleeing Vietnamese civilians to prevent their murder."[1]

Thompson spent many years speaking at military bases about the moral and legal responsibilities of soldiers on the battlefield. As he stated in 2004, "Don't do the right thing looking for a reward, because it might not come."[2]

1. Quoted in Richard Goldstein, "Hugh Thompson, 62, Who Saved Civilians at My Lai, Dies," *New York Times*, January 7, 2006. www.nytimes.com/2006/01/07/us/hugh-thompson-62-who-saved-civilians-at-my-lai-dies.html.
2. Quoted in Goldstein, "Hugh Thompson, 62, Who Saved Civilians at My Lai, Dies."

A Lethal Protest

Once the public saw the photographs of the dead at My Lai and learned the grim details of the killings in late 1969, support for the war eroded steadily. By August 1971, 61 percent of respondents to a Gallup poll called for an immediate withdrawal of troops from Vietnam. This marked the first time that a majority of Americans opposed the war.

The protests continued. In August 1969, nearly 500,000 young people gathered near the New York State town of Bethel for the Woodstock Music and Art Festival. The three-day rock concert turned into a giant anti-war rally. Performer after performer included political messages in between their songs. Later that year, 250,000 young Americans marched on Washington, demanding an end to the war.

On May 4, 1970, an anti-war protest at Ohio's Kent State University turned violent. The students and other anti-war activists who gathered for the

Members of the National Guard can be seen here chasing students at Kent State University after an anti-war protest turned violent.

rally were met by National Guardsmen. When some students started pelting the soldiers with stones, the guardsmen retreated—at first. However, then they turned and began firing on the protesters. Four students were killed, and nine were wounded. Americans were shocked when they saw photographs of the incident—one famous picture depicted a distraught teenage girl next to the body of a dead student— and the shootings sparked protests at other campuses.

Facing Complications

As anti-war protests continued in the United States, soldiers were returning home from Vietnam and finding that some Americans did not see them as heroes. With the war losing support, veterans were easy targets for criticism. Anti-war protesters criticized the soldiers and called them names. Many veterans later admitted that such treatment made returning to civilian life very difficult.

These soldiers also suffered from psychological and physical problems related to their service. One of the more common complications was post-traumatic stress disorder (PTSD). This psychological condition is triggered by stressful episodes in a person's life. It can manifest itself through nightmares, insomnia, flashbacks, memory loss, depression, and other mental conditions. Some veterans found themselves acting irrationally when they suddenly remembered a stressful memory from their Vietnam service. Following the war, studies showed that as many as 30 percent of Vietnam veterans suffered at least one incident of PTSD.

Aside from PTSD, other problems afflicted veterans. About 100,000 Americans were disabled to some degree by wounds received in the war. Additionally, some veterans later contracted cancer and other illnesses because they had been exposed to Agent Orange during their tours in Vietnam. Agent Orange is a chemical used to defoliate jungles. It was sprayed in abundance to burn the heavy foliage away from villages, military bases, and other installations to deny hiding places to Viet Cong guerrillas.

Another problem that many Vietnam veterans later had to deal with was hepatitis C, a blood disease. Hepatitis C has long been widespread in Southeast Asia. Medical researchers have concluded that soldiers who received blood transfusions during the war may have been infected with hepatitis C because of the unsanitary conditions on the battlefields. It can take up to 30 years for the disease to emerge, but eventually, it can lead to liver failure and death.

Life as a POW

The veterans who returned home had to cope with challenges, but other servicemen found themselves virtually forgotten. They were prisoners of war (POWs) held by the North Vietnamese in cramped, dark, and unsanitary camps

American planes , such as the one shown here, sprayed the chemical Agent Orange to kill the dense foliage in Vietnam and prevent the Viet Cong from hiding in it.

or jails. Most POWs were pilots who had been shot down while on bombing missions over the North. These prisoners were fed just enough food to keep them alive. They were subjected to constant beatings and other torture. Some were led through Vietnamese city streets as people yelled and threw stones at them.

In 1969, reports started leaking out about North Vietnam's brutal treatment of prisoners. Some unfortunate pilots were held for months or even years in "tiger cages." These bamboo cages were often too small to stand in. Most other prisoners were held in more than a dozen filthy, rat-infested prisons in the North. Guards beat and interrogated them. Most POWs were forced to sign propaganda statements or appear in crude films claiming their bombing missions had been criminal acts.

Pilots frequently were injured when they were shot down, suffering broken bones and other wounds. When they were captured, the North Vietnamese provided only the most basic medical care. North Vietnamese doctors set broken bones but used no painkillers. Infections were common, as were diseases contracted in the jungle or in prison, including malaria (a mosquito-borne disease that causes people to suffer from chills, fever, and flu-like symptoms) and dysentery (an intestinal disease resulting in severe stomach pain and diarrhea). Food was commonly issued in tiny portions of rice, noodles, and watery soup.

U.S. prisoners of war captured by the North Vietnamese endured terrible living conditions in crude accommodations, such as the prison shown here.

WAR CRIMINALS?

During the First Indochina War in 1949, North Vietnam had signed the Geneva Conventions, a treaty that said prisoners of war were to be treated humanely. During the Vietnam War, the North Vietnamese at first insisted that American prisoners were being held under humane conditions. They showcased POWs at a prison known as the Plantation, formerly a mansion occupied by the mayor of Hanoi. The facility had clean cells and gardens tilled by the inmates. Whenever foreign human rights dignitaries demanded to see the POW conditions in North Vietnam, they were given tours of the Plantation.

However, when news of the true prison conditions leaked out, the Communists assumed a new stance. They insisted that since America had never formally declared war on North Vietnam, the Americans were not prisoners of war. Instead, they were war criminals. The rationale had little effect. The North Vietnamese came under intense international pressure to improve conditions for the POWs. Eventually, the prisoners' food and medical care improved, and the torture ceased.

Interrogations were routine in the North Vietnamese prisons. Interrogators wanted to know about American war plans and military organization. When the pilots refused to talk, they were tortured. Navy pilot John McCain, who died in 2018, would later become a senator from Arizona. He was captured in 1967 when his plane was shot down over Hanoi. He broke a leg and both arms in the crash and spent six years as a POW. McCain described his experience in an interrogation room:

At two-to-three-hour intervals, the guards returned to administer beatings. The intensity of the punishment varied from visit to visit depending on the energy and enthusiasm of the guards. Still, I felt they were being careful not to kill or permanently injure me. One guard would hold me while the others pounded away. Most blows were directed at my shoulders, chest, and stomach. Occasionally, when I had fallen to the floor, they kicked me in the head. They cracked several of my ribs and broke a couple of teeth. My bad right leg was swollen and hurt the most of any of my injuries. Weakened by beatings and dysentery, and with my right leg again nearly useless, I found it almost impossible to stand.[22]

Unlike many of the soldiers who returned from Vietnam, McCain and 590 other POWs released by the North

Vietnamese in early 1973 came home to a warm embrace by Americans. The plight of these prisoners had become well known in the United States. Now, Americans were anxious to show their appreciation to the veterans who had endured the worst of the war. McCain recalled,

During our captivity, the Vietnamese had inundated us with information about how unpopular the war and the men who fought it had become with the American public. We were stunned and relieved to discover that most Americans were as happy to see us as we were to see them. A lot of us were overcome by our reception, and the affection we were shown helped us to begin putting the war behind us.[23]

POWs finally able to return to the United States were greeted by welcoming crowds in 1973.

CHAPTER FOUR

TALK OF PEACE

By May 10, 1968, it seemed as if peace between North Vietnam and the United States might be in the near future. Diplomats from both sides had agreed to meet in Paris to negotiate terms. Was this long and bloody war finally grinding to a halt? It was a historic moment, and the world was watching.

Unfortunately, it did not last. The meeting began with a hopeful attitude as everyone sat down at the bargaining table, but it was quickly shattered by anger, hostility, and misunderstandings. The North Vietnamese were unwilling to recognize the South Vietnamese government as legitimate, and South Vietnam refused to accept the North Vietnamese government. Both sides clung to their demands without offering a compromise. It soon became clear that neither side was about to give an inch. Despite numerous meetings over the next few months, no solution emerged.

A Bitter Campaign

In the wake of this failed peace attempt, in 1968, Americans endured a bitter campaign for the presidency. Vice President Hubert Humphrey won the Democratic nomination. Although he had no choice but to support the war as part of the Johnson administration, in the final weeks of his campaign, he called for a halt to all bombing in the North.

The Republican nominee was Richard Nixon, a former vice president and fierce anti-Communist who insisted he had a secret plan to end the war. As more peace talks got underway in Paris in October, Nixon sent an emissary to South Vietnamese president Nguyen Van Thieu, urging Thieu not to participate in the negotiations. Handwritten notes taken by Nixon's aide and future chief of staff H. R. Haldeman have proven that Nixon wanted to put a "monkey wrench"[24] into the negotiations so Humphrey would not edge him out in the election.

The emissary assured Thieu that South Vietnam would get a better deal from Nixon than from either Johnson or Humphrey. Thieu agreed to Nixon's proposal. South Vietnam stayed out of the talks. Without their participation, any hope for a quick resolution in Paris was doomed.

As the U.S. presidential campaign continued, Nixon's lead was threatened by the people's enthusiasm for Humphrey's plan to end the war. Humphrey's popularity, however, was also dimmed by those who were tired of how the Democrats had handled the war so far. The election ended in a narrow victory for Nixon. Experts believe many anti-war voters simply stayed home on Election Day. They likely felt that neither Humphrey nor Nixon would agree to an immediate stop to the hostilities.

Richard Nixon (right) became the 37th president of the United States on January 20, 1969.

Contrary to what Nixon had announced during his campaign, he had no secret plan to end the war. He had been vice president during the final year of the Korean War and had seen President Eisenhower threaten to use nuclear weapons on the North Koreans unless they agreed to a cease-fire. The strategy had worked. Now, Nixon intended to use virtually the same approach on the North Vietnamese. He would threaten them with nuclear weapons and increase the bombing in the North to force the Communists to submit to his terms. Nixon explained the strategy to Haldeman:

> I call it the Madman Theory ... I want the North Vietnamese to believe that I've reached the point where I might do anything to stop the war. We'll just slip the word to them that, "for God's sake, you know Nixon is obsessed about Communists. We can't restrain him when he's angry—and he has his hand on the nuclear button"—and Ho Chi Minh himself will be in Paris in two days begging for peace.[25]

As Nixon stepped up the bombing campaign in the North, he also began following through on a campaign promise to withdraw American troops and return the war to the South Vietnamese. Shortly after Nixon's election, there were around 500,000 soldiers in Vietnam. A year later, the force had dropped by 60,000 men, and further reductions followed.

Communist Arrests

While the United States continued its air support for the ARVN and an intense bombing campaign in the North, some American advisors also aided the South Vietnamese in a series of arrests of suspected Communists, known as the Phoenix Program.

The program began in 1968, following the Tet Offensive. Under direction from the CIA, South Vietnamese agents—most drafted from rural villages—started scouring the countryside, rounding up suspected Viet Cong guerrillas and their civilian sympathizers. At first, the program offered amnesty to the Viet Cong. Those who turned themselves and their weapons in would go free. Many guerrillas surrendered under those terms.

Soon, though, the South Vietnamese agents became much more aggressive in tracking down guerrillas. They resorted to extremist tactics such as torture and assassination to expose Viet Cong guerrillas. Eventually, more than 300,000 suspected guerrillas were targeted, with many thrown into jails or makeshift prison camps. Some were murdered while in custody. Others who were arrested were falsely accused of collaborating with the Communists. "When you grab that many bodies, you grab a lot of the wrong bodies," insisted Barton Osborne, a U.S. Army intelligence officer. "By late 1968, the Phoenix Program was not serving any legitimate function that I know of, but rather had gone so wrong that it was

A unit of South Vietnamese operatives can be seen here holding a flag of the Viet Cong, who were captured during the Phoenix Program with increasingly aggressive tactics.

the vehicle by which we were getting into a bad genocide program."[26]

THE PROBLEM OF DRUGS

American soldiers stationed in South Vietnam had little trouble obtaining illegal drugs. Marijuana was readily available from street dealers in Saigon and other cities—so were other drugs, including heroin, opium, methamphetamines (also known as speed), and lysergic acid diethylamide (LSD or acid).

Army private George Cantero recalled the ease with which he could obtain drugs in an article for PBS: "For a box of Tide [laundry detergent], you could get a carton of pre-packed, pre-rolled marijuana cigarettes soaked in opium," he said. "For ten dollars you could get a vial of pure heroin. You could get liquid opium, speed, acid, anything you wanted."[1]

In 1971, a study authorized by Congress found that drugs had become a major problem in the military, undermining the ability of many units to fight. The study estimated that roughly 30,000 American soldiers serving in Vietnam were addicted to heroin.

1. Quoted in American Experience, "Vietnam Online," PBS, accessed on September 14, 2018. www.shoppbs.org/wgbh/amex/vietnam/series/pt_01.html.

An Increased Willingness?

Even as U.S. ground troops withdrew, Nixon tested his madman theory by sending a message to officials in the North. He threatened an even more massive bombing campaign unless they agreed to withdraw their claims on the South. On September 2, 1969, while Communist leaders considered the ramifications of Nixon's threat, Ho Chi Minh died at the age of 79. Congress used this event to urge Nixon to engage in serious peace talks with the North. Many of them felt that Ho's death offered a great opportunity for peace because a new generation of North Vietnamese leaders might be more willing to give ground.

The North Vietnamese mourned the death of the beloved "Uncle Ho." On the day he died, the Communist government released a statement that Ho had written a few months earlier, urging the North Vietnamese people to endure the air strikes. The statement read, in part,

> Our compatriots in the North and the South shall be reunited under the same roof. We, a small nation, will have earned the unique honor of defeating, through a heroic struggle, two big imperialisms—the French and the American—and making a worthy contribution to the national liberation movement … To the whole people, the whole [Communist] party, the whole army, to my nephews and nieces, the youth and children, I leave my boundless love.[27]

After Ho's death, the North proved no more willing to give in than before. North Vietnamese leaders steadfastly refused to give ground. Nixon's plan was not working. Public opinion in America remained overwhelmingly against the war, but Nixon was not ready to give up. He believed he could bomb the enemy into submission. In 1969 he told members of Congress, "I will not be the first president of the United States to lose a war."[28] Nixon stepped up the bombings, and the war went on.

Crossing Borders

For years, Cambodia and Laos had been indirectly involved in the Vietnam War. The Ho Chi Minh Trail crossed their territories, making them strategically

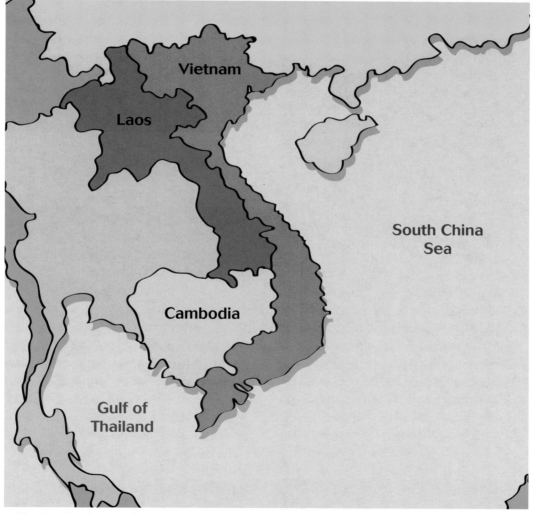

Sharing borders with Vietnam meant Laos and Cambodia shared the ongoing conflict.

important. Cambodia's leader, Prince Norodom Sihanouk, had negotiated with China, France, Indonesia, and other countries to maintain neutrality during the conflict. However, by 1969, the North Vietnamese army and Viet Cong had established bases along Cambodia's 500-mile (805 km) border with South Vietnam, using them to launch attacks on the South. In an effort to keep the war confined to Vietnam, however, the United States had not attacked enemy positions in Cambodia.

Nixon threw aside this strategy. He was convinced that if he took out these Cambodian bases, he could seriously hamper the ability of the Viet Cong and North Vietnamese army to attack the South. In 1969, Nixon secretly ordered bombing raids on targets in Cambodia. Then, on April 30, 1970, he sent American ground troops into Cambodia.

On the surface, the intense military campaign was effective, forcing the North Vietnamese to shut down their bases along the border. However, instead of driving the Communists back to the North, the military campaign pushed them farther into Cambodia. There, they could assist a group of insurgents who were trying to topple Sihanouk's government. Eventually, a group known as the Khmer Rouge won a guerrilla war in Cambodia and plunged the country into one of the most horrific periods of genocide in world history.

Meanwhile, Laos faced its own insurgency. The United States had been carrying on a secret war in Laos since the early 1960s. The country was governed by a shaky coalition that included members of the Pathet Lao, the Communist organization in Laos. In the countryside, Pathet Lao guerrillas armed by the North Vietnamese battled Hmong tribesmen, who were armed by the CIA. The CIA ferried arms and supplies to the Hmong and conducted air reconnaissance missions with planes from a phony airline it had set up in Asia. The Hmong tribesmen managed to fight the Pathet Lao to a stalemate until the early 1970s.

Unfortunately, the Laotian military, the Royal Lao Army, was largely ineffective. As a result, the Communists had free rein to establish camps along South Vietnam's border with Laos. In early 1971, South Vietnamese and American troops started conducting raids into Laos, driving the Communists into the interior. Communist troops based in Laos would cease to pose a threat to South Vietnam, but the Pathet Lao soon became a dominant force in Laos.

In the United States, anti-war activists criticized Nixon for spreading the war into Laos and Cambodia after proclaiming for months that he was seeking an end to the conflict. Congress also demanded an end to the bombing of Cambodia. In response, Nixon insisted that he was ending the war. The evidence was in the thousands of soldiers coming home. By the end of 1970, American troop strength in South Vietnam was reduced to 280,000 soldiers.

As U.S. troops departed, the South Vietnamese army was left to carry on the fight. Nixon called this transfer of responsibility "Vietnamization." By the late 1960s, the strength of the South Vietnamese army stood at 1 million members, although their numbers were threatened by the 2,000 who deserted each week. Once the Americans started withdrawing ground troops, however, the South Vietnamese soldiers responded with courage and fortitude.

Rangers in the South Vietnamese army regularly patrolled the country's border with Cambodia, looking for Viet Cong guerrillas.

CELEBRITY TOURS

Throughout World War II and the Korean War, American comedian Bob Hope had performed variety shows at American military outposts. The nine Christmas-season shows he produced for soldiers in South Vietnam from 1964 to 1972 made Hope into an American icon, especially since these shows were broadcast on American television.

The shows always opened with Hope strutting onto the stage. He told jokes about American politicians, military leaders, and others in the news. He was fol-

lowed by a cast of singers, dancers, and other performers, including such stars of the time as Ann-Margret, Raquel Welch, Phyllis Diller, Lola Falana, and Jim Nabors. Baseball star Johnny Bench and astronaut Neil Armstrong also made appearances.

Chicago newspaper columnist Irv Kupcinet once described Hope as "Uncle Sam, Santa Claus and a letter from home all wrapped up in one neat package of hilarity."[1] Many years after the Vietnam War, in 1990, at the age of 87, Hope organized a tour of military installations in Saudi Arabia as the United States prepared to oust the Iraqis from Kuwait in Operation Desert Storm. Hope died in 2003 at age 100.

Actor and comedian Bob Hope is shown here entertaining U.S. troops in a 1965 appearance.

1. Quoted in Timothy M. Gray and Richard Natale, "Hope and Joy," *Variety*, August 4, 2003. variety.com/1992/more/news/with-hope-it-was-rarely-quiet-on-the-front-102247/.

Permission to Publish

In 1971, public opinion turned even more sharply against Nixon as secret facts about the war were revealed. In June, the *New York Times* and *Washington Post* began publishing portions of a 7,000-page State Department report that had been leaked to reporters by Daniel Ellsberg, a former State Department official. The report, known as the Pentagon Papers, chronicled the 30-year history of America's involvement in Vietnam. It indicated that President Johnson had escalated the war into Laos as far back as 1964, ordering air strikes and ground attacks long before Nixon publicly acknowledged attacking Communist positions in Laos in 1971. Other previously unknown missions by American troops were also reported. The papers suggested that Johnson had decided to commit the full might of the American military to Vietnam within the first few months of the conflict, when many U.S. officials believed a diplomatic solution to the crisis still was possible.

Nixon moved quickly to stop the release of more of the Pentagon Papers. Although he had not been in office during the period they covered, he feared that revelations concerning the early days of the war would turn the public further against continuing the fight. Insisting that publication of the papers would endanger America's foreign policy, he asked the newspapers not to publish them. Both newspapers refused, but U.S. Attorney General John Mitchell won a court order prohibiting publication. Within days, however, the U.S. Supreme Court ruled that the Nixon administration had no right to tell a newspaper what it could and could not publish. The newspapers resumed publishing the Pentagon Papers. It was a tremendous victory for freedom of the press in the United States.

Nixon was willing to use the full power of the law to promote his agenda, however. Days after the Pentagon Papers were leaked, the president ordered the U.S. Department of Justice to charge Ellsberg with conspiracy, theft, and violations of espionage statutes. The charges were eventually dismissed after evidence of government misconduct against Ellsberg came out.

Bitter Talks, Bitter Fighting

Soon after the publication of the Pentagon Papers, President Thieu won re-election in South Vietnam. The United States continued to support Thieu, even though his status was a major stumbling block in the Paris peace talks. The North Vietnamese refused to deal with Thieu, insisting he resign and another leader take control. However, Nixon and his chief negotiator, National Security Advisor Henry Kissinger, resisted. They knew that any president approved by the North Vietnamese would surely be a puppet of the Hanoi regime. They refused to allow Thieu to be ousted from power.

On March 30, 1972, the Communists initiated the largest offensive since Tet in 1968. Approximately 120,000 North

Brutal fighting in and around Quang Tri City left the area nearly destroyed.

Vietnamese and Viet Cong troops attacked 3 strategic regions of South Vietnam: An Loc in the south; the Central Highlands; and the province of Quang Tri in the north.

The most intense fighting was in Quang Tri. Refugees streamed out of the province and its capital, Quang Tri City. The government of South Vietnam rushed troops north. They were aided by U.S. air power, but no American ground troops participated in the battle. By then, only about 70,000 American soldiers remained in Vietnam.

At first, the Communists took the city and surrounding province. Then, after fighting for more than five months, on September 15, the South Vietnamese recaptured the capital. American air power had been instrumental in rooting out the enemy. One reporter who toured Quang Tri after it was retaken by the South said the city had been virtually destroyed in the bombing campaign. Quang Tri, the reporter wrote, "is no longer a city but a lake of masonry. Even the thick citadel walls were so thoroughly smashed one could no longer see where they had stood."[29] The casualties reflected the changing dynamic of the fighting: More than 5,000 South Vietnamese soldiers lost their lives, but not a single American was killed.

Breakthroughs

Throughout the first months of 1972, Nixon looked for global allies for support in ending the war. In February, he traveled to China, becoming the first American president to visit the country since the Communist takeover in 1949. A few months later, Nixon visited the Soviet Union. He had met with officials in the two countries with the most influence over North Vietnam.

In China, Nixon found the country's leaders receptive to talks for ending the war. The Chinese had long been wary of the Soviets. They wanted the United States to remain a presence in South Vietnam to keep the Soviet Union in check. They feared that if the Americans left, the Soviets would dominate Vietnam and establish bases along the Vietnam and China border, putting them in a position to exert more power over China.

The Soviets had their own reasons to cooperate with U.S. efforts. They were concerned about the nuclear arms race with the United States and desperately wanted to discuss a treaty to limit nuclear proliferation. To obtain the treaty, Soviet officials indicated they would press the North Vietnamese to agree to a cease-fire. In May 1972, Nixon announced a new series of bombings in the North as well as the mining (the exploding of underwater mines) of Haiphong harbor in North Vietnam. Such an action would hamper North Vietnamese war efforts, but it would also endanger Soviet shipping. When the Soviets raised no more than a token protest about the mining, Nixon knew the pieces had fallen into place to end the war.

President Nixon is shown here with Chinese
Premier Zhou Enlai in 1972.

DESTRUCTION FROM WITHIN

During the final years of the Vietnam War, some American officers were targeted by their own men. Often these officers were new to the war and had arrived in camp eager to lead missions into the jungle. Many of the enlisted men, seasoned through months of battle, found the new officers incompetent and reckless. By then, morale was low among many of the troops, who wanted nothing more than to go home.

In *The Ten Thousand Day War*, Michael Maclear quoted Vietnam veteran Mike Beaman:

> We used to refuse certain missions because we thought they were brutal. If I didn't want to go in a certain direction, if I felt that we were going to have a confrontation and shoot people for no reason at all, other than to get a body count, I'd say, 'No ... I'm going this way. You, officer, can go that way, but the other people will follow me.'[1]

Poor leadership and flagging morale sometimes led to soldiers victimizing their officers in attacks known as fragging. They would roll a fragmentation grenade (one with a casing that shattered into many destructive pieces when detonated) into the tent of a sleeping officer or other leader. Between 1969 and 1972, 86 officers and noncommissioned officers were killed in fragging incidents. Another 714 sustained wounds.

In addition to these deliberate killings, about 15 percent of all U.S. casualties in the war were attributed to friendly fire, meaning the soldiers were killed or wounded by shots fired from their own ranks. While most of the friendly fire incidents were accidental, military investigators believe some of the shootings were intentional.

1. Quoted in Michael Maclear, *The Ten Thousand Day War: Vietnam, 1945–1975.* New York, NY: St. Martin's, 1981, p. 271.

Operation Linebacker II

As Nixon and the United States planned new attacks, the peace talks dragged on with little progress. Then, on October 26, 1972, after a series of intense talks, Kissinger and chief North Vietnamese negotiator Le Duc Tho emerged from a meeting in Paris. Kissinger announced, "We believe peace is at hand."[30] Again, his optimism came too soon. After another month and a half of talks, negotiations fell apart completely on December 13, 1972. Diplomats on both sides were angry and frustrated. Nixon responded with aggression, organizing Operation Linebacker II. Starting on December 18, in what became known as the Christmas bombing, American planes dropped more than 20,000 tons (18,143.7 mt) of bombs on the cities of Hanoi and Haiphong. The attacks continued until December 28, when North Vietnam finally agreed to resume peace talks.

Finally, in January 1973, a peace agreement was signed. It did not fully unify Vietnam, however. Instead, it recognized Vietnam as one country with two distinct governments. While

American B-52 bombers conducted intense air raids on North Vietnam during Operation Linebacker II in December 1972.

President Thieu would remain in power in South Vietnam, both sides would work toward a political settlement to allow the Vietnamese people to decide their future through free elections. Other terms of the agreement said that American combat troops would withdraw from South Vietnam and that the North Vietnamese would release American prisoners.

In addition, the defense of South Vietnam would be turned over to the ARVN, but North Vietnamese troops already camped in the South would be permitted to hold their positions. Thieu balked at that condition and at first refused to sign the agreement, but eventually, he bowed to intense pressure from the United States and agreed to the terms.

While imperfect, the peace agreement was an important start. However, by that time, Nixon was facing other problems at home—ones that would profoundly impact the war.

CHAPTER FIVE

BROKEN PROMISES

Following the peace talks, President Nixon made a promise to South Vietnam: If the North violated the terms of the cease-fire negotiated by Henry Kissinger and Le Duc Tho, the United States would return to help. However, even promises made in good faith can be broken. In 1972, Nixon became involved in a scandal known as Watergate, which resulted in his eventual resignation in 1974. The promise he had made to South Vietnam collapsed along with his presidency.

The Watergate Scandal

Nixon's presidency started unraveling on the night of June 17, 1972. Five burglars were caught inside the office of the Democratic National Committee in the Watergate hotel and office complex in Washington, D.C., with electronic eavesdropping equipment. They had intended to set up the equipment and place the office under surveillance. Later, as the Watergate scandal unfolded, it was revealed that operatives working for Nixon's reelection committee had hired the burglars. They had hoped to find damaging information about the Democrats, especially Senator George McGovern, Nixon's opponent in the fall election. At first, the White House downplayed the importance of the incident. Shortly after the break-in, Nixon's press secretary, Ron Ziegler, dismissed it as a "third-rate burglary attempt."[31]

Eventually, though, the Watergate details became public, and it became clear the burglary was merely one small piece of a widespread campaign intended to guarantee Nixon's reelection in 1972. Another part of the plan included sending a team of burglars into the office of the psychiatrist of Daniel Ellsberg, the former State Department official who had leaked the Pentagon Papers. The burglars were planning to use Ellsberg's psychological records to discredit him.

*As the details of Watergate
became public, people began to
call for Nixon's impeachment.*

In November 1972, the public did not know about the Watergate scandal yet, and Nixon was reelected. However, by 1973, Watergate had gained national attention. Congress convened hearings on the scandal. Witnesses testified that Nixon and his aides had resorted to dirty politics partially because they were afraid of opponents of the war gaining popular support. If that happened, they could force the White House into accepting a foreign policy favoring North Vietnam.

Fighting the Truth

As journalists, prosecutors, and members of Congress probed for the truth, Nixon fought back. He battled the accusations against him and tried to keep White House records— particularly audiotapes of his Oval Office conversations—out of the hands of prosecutors. The scandal would have a tremendous bearing on American activity in Vietnam.

Years later, Kissinger stated the Watergate scandal was a decisive factor in South Vietnam's fall. The president, fighting against congressional inquiries set up to find the truth about Watergate, was not in a position to ask Congress to send troops back to Southeast Asia. In fact, according to Kissinger, the North Vietnamese were following the progress of the Watergate hearings closely themselves. They had come to the conclusion that Nixon had been weakened politically and could never muster support in Congress to send ground troops, or even air support, back to South Vietnam. Seeing an opportunity, the Communists started planning to attack the South. Kissinger later wrote,

After June 1973 I did not believe that the cease-fire would hold. Watergate was in full swing. We had already acquired intelligence documents in which the North Vietnamese had made the very correct analysis that Nixon would not be in a position to repeat [the bombing of] 1972, because of his domestic difficulties. The congressional agitation to end all military activities in Southeast Asia was already in full force.[32]

Unable to keep the incriminating tapes away from prosecutors, and facing certain impeachment in Congress, Nixon resigned on August 9, 1974. By then, the Communists had built up troops along their border with the South. They had sent 100,000 soldiers and their equipment down the Ho Chi Minh Trail, now a paved highway. Meanwhile, Thieu was losing control of his government. The livelihoods of millions of South Vietnamese, who had worked as maids, cab drivers, shoe shiners, secretaries, and thousands of other roles, had depended on the American soldiers. Once the Americans left, these incomes dried up. The South Vietnamese economy was in shambles.

The government in South Vietnam was also running out of money. Thieu found it difficult to pay the army. As a result, morale was low among South Vietnamese soldiers. The leadership of the ARVN was generally regarded as corrupt. Bribery, embezzlement, and robbery occurred in the ranks. Some helicopter pilots insisted on bribes to evacuate the wounded. At the time, the United States was still supplying the South Vietnamese army with $1 billion a year in aid. Little of it filtered down to the rank-and-file soldiers.

A Swift Takeover

Without U.S. soldiers to support them, the ARVN was outmatched by the North Vietnamese army. The Communists, sensing their advantage, began with minor skirmishing against South Vietnamese troops in December 1974 as a diversionary tactic. This drew attention away from a major offensive against Phuoc Long City, located along the Cambodian border about 62 miles (100 km) west of Saigon. Phuoc Long City fell on January 6, 1975. It was a decisive victory for the North Vietnamese. They had planned for a two-year campaign. Instead, the sweep took only a few months.

Despite the slaughter of the South Vietnamese troops, the United States stayed on the sidelines. Although the new American president, Gerald R. Ford, had reiterated Nixon's

Before Gerald Ford was president, he served as Richard Nixon's vice president until Nixon's resignation.

commitment not to abandon Thieu, he was also unable to keep that promise. Ford was convinced that with American air support, the South Vietnamese could at least fight the North to a stalemate. In the meantime, Ford planned to send diplomats back to Vietnam to negotiate a new cease-fire. He asked Congress to commit another $722 million to the South and to resume air support for their troops, but Congress refused. Millicent Fenwick, a member of Congress from New Jersey, explained why she was against the spending: "We've sent, so to speak, battleship after battleship, and bomber after bomber, and 500,000 or more men, and billions and billions of dollars. If billions and billions didn't do at a time when we had all our men there, how can $722 million save the day?"[33]

Cities Fall

Fierce fighting broke out in other places. After taking Phuoc Long, the Communists targeted the Central Highlands. Under the command of General Van Tien Dung, on March 1, the North Vietnamese attacked the city of Ban Me Thuot. The general ordered it to be pummeled with artillery and then sent 80,000 soldiers to face the same number of South Vietnamese defenders. While defending Ban Me Thuot, South Vietnamese commander General Pham Van Phu made a mistake. He believed the main assault would occur against the nearby city of Pleiku, so he shifted most of his forces there. Dung fed Phu's belief, sending a diversionary force against Pleiku, but the real thrust of the attack was aimed at Ban Me Thuot, which was now an easy target.

The South Vietnamese soldiers resisted and managed to hold out until March 12, when the city finally fell. Thieu ordered Phu to try to retake the city, but the South Vietnamese suffered from miscommunications and mistakes from their leaders. Tank and artillery support arrived too late. The army was plagued by desertions. Many of the defenders had families in Ban Me Thuot and broke ranks to try to find them. According to General Phillip B. Davidson, who headed U.S. Army intelligence in Vietnam, "While the battle of Phuoc Long marked a major turning point in the Indochina War … by demonstrating the impotence of both the ARVN and the United States, it was the ARVN's loss at Ban Me Thuot which marked the beginning of the end for the Republic of Vietnam."[34]

The Central Highlands city of Pleiku fell next. That battle produced tens of thousands of refugees who made their way east to the port city of Da Nang. There, they hoped to buy passage on ships to South Vietnam or even to safe harbors in other countries. Many of the refugees were South Vietnamese soldiers, who had thrown away their weapons, stripped off their uniforms, and joined their families. Thousands of refugees did escape, but thousands more were forced to stay behind. Just north of Da Nang, Hue fell on March 26. Da Nang fell five days later.

The Final Glory

The final moment of glory for the ARVN occurred at Xuan Loc, east of Saigon. Already depleted by casualties and desertions, a mere 5,000 South Vietnamese soldiers remained to defend the city. General Dung committed 40,000 North Vietnamese army soldiers to the battle. Fighting broke out on April 9. Despite incurring heavy losses, the South Vietnamese fought hard and killed more than 5,000 of the enemy. The defenders held out until April 22 but finally collapsed under the North's superior numbers and firepower.

A day after Xuan Loc fell, President Thieu resigned and fled to Taiwan. He was succeeded by Vice President Tran Van Huong, an aging, nearly blind bureaucrat. Communist leaders sent word to the South that Huong was an unacceptable choice. In Saigon, government leaders met to name a new leader whom they believed could negotiate with the Communists. They selected Duong Van Minh, a former South Vietnamese army general who had long opposed the Thieu regime. On April 28, Huong resigned, and Minh took his place.

In Saigon, chaos, looting, and a rush to escape marked the last days of April 1975. By that point, virtually the only way out of the country was by helicopter. At noon on April 29, Armed Forces Radio started playing a recording of Bing Crosby's song "White Christmas" many times in a row. Americans knew that was the signal to get out. They made their way to the U.S. embassy, which was still in operation. During the final two days of the month, hundreds of helicopters were dispatched from U.S. aircraft carriers in the South China Sea. They landed on the embassy roof, airlifting embassy staff members, businessmen, journalists, aid workers, and other Americans to safety.

Next, the American military evacuated as many South Vietnamese citizens as possible. Those given priority were Vietnamese government officials, military leaders, and others who had worked closely with the Americans. Their lives were at the most risk from the Communists. South Vietnamese general Tran Van Don recalled the final chaotic hours. He said, "Nobody at the embassy told me what to do—just go to the gate, they said ... People were shouting, 'That's General Don—follow him. He can leave. He knows the way out, for sure.'"[35] Don was on one of the last helicopters to leave Saigon. Over the course of 19 hours, more than 1,000 Americans and 5,000 Vietnamese were flown out of the city on 81 helicopters. Many other South Vietnamese boarded primitive, overcrowded boats and sailed into the South China Sea. They were later rescued by navy ships cruising offshore.

When North Vietnamese army tanks rolled into Saigon on the morning of April 30, they were surprised to find how quiet and empty the streets were. Earlier, Minh had told his troops to lay down their arms and not resist.

Many South Vietnamese refugees, such as the ones shown here, narrowly escaped the fall of Saigon in 1975.

A single tank crashed through the gates of Independence Palace, and a soldier jumped out. He climbed to the upstairs balcony, where, in a dramatic gesture, he unfurled the flag of the Communist nation. Saigon would soon be renamed Ho Chi Minh City. Inside the palace, Colonel Bui Tin accepted Saigon's surrender. He stated,

When I saw fear on the faces of Minh and the others present, I said, "The

Today, the Reunification Palace in Ho Chi Minh City features replicas of the tanks that were in use at the end of the Vietnam War.

war has ended today, and all Vietnamese are victors. Only the American imperialists are the vanquished. If you still have any feelings for the nation and the people, consider today a happy day."

That night, when I sprawled on the lawn of the Independence Palace with members of a communication unit, we all agreed it was the happiest day of our lives because it was a day of complete victory for the nation, because the war ended.[36]

LESSONS LEARNED

The war left deep scars on Vietnam. Millions of Vietnamese—an estimated 10 percent of the country's population—either died or were injured. Thousands of South Vietnamese who had held government or military positions were imprisoned by the North Vietnamese. Independent businesses were shut down. It was little surprise that more than 1 million Vietnamese fled the country by the early 1990s.

Years of warfare also left Vietnam with an infrastructure crushed to rubble by bombing attacks and with an environment severely damaged by chemical weapons. These problems, coupled with economic sanctions imposed by the United States, left the country's economy in ruins.

Still, Vietnam was not finished fighting. Neighboring Cambodia was overrun by the Communist Khmer Rouge regime. More than 1.5 million people had been killed in a genocidal takeover.

It only ended when the Vietnamese army stepped in and drove the Khmer Rouge out of power. The Vietnamese also had to repel an invasion by China in 1979.

Today, Vietnam is still a Communist country. Its people suffer from government oppression and restricted rights and freedoms. However, as time has passed, Communism no longer holds the same level of international threat that it did during the 1950s and 1960s. The Cold War ended in 1991 when the Soviet Union collapsed, marking the downfall of a major Communist power. Additionally, while other countries—notably China—have remained Communist, perspectives have changed and the grip of ideology has relaxed somewhat. For example, eager to build its economy, China has opened its doors to free-market trading and become a global economic power.

While the war impacted Vietnam dramatically, it had little lasting effect

Many of Vietnam's villages were burned or destroyed from years of war. Rebuilding was slow and difficult.

on the world overall. The fears expressed by American politicians about the international spread of Communism proved, in hindsight, to be unfounded. However, back in 1945, the United States could not bring itself to support a Communist government under any circumstances.

Trouble in Cambodia

After the war, Vietnam struggled to establish its political position in Southeast Asia. Already, trouble was brewing on its western border with Cambodia and on its northern border with China.

Led by Pol Pot, the Khmer Rouge seized power in 1975 in Cambodia. For the next four years, the Khmer Rouge tried to turn the country into a society of communal farms. Hundreds of thousands of citizens were driven out of their homes and forced to live on these small farms. Many who did not cooperate were murdered. This scheme to remake the country failed, however, and hundreds of thousands died from starvation. By 1979, it was estimated that more than 1.5 million Cambodians died under the Khmer Rouge regime. When the regime started targeting Vietnamese living in Cambodia and also began making incursions across the border into Vietnam, the Vietnamese military stepped in. They invaded Cambodia to oust the Khmer Rouge. Pol Pot and his allies were chased into the jungle, where they hid for years. In the meantime, a United Nations peacekeeping force worked to stabilize the country, and eventually, a democracy emerged. Even today, though, occasional fighting still breaks out in Cambodia. Its government is considered one of the most corrupt in the world.

In 1975, the Vietnamese-backed Pathet Lao signed a treaty with the government of Laos giving the Communist organization tremendous influence over the country. The Pathet Lao ran the government of Laos until 1990. Soon after gaining power, in 1977, a treaty allowed Vietnam to house a large contingent of troops in Laos, essentially making the smaller country into a Vietnamese colony. Eventually, the Pathet Lao disbanded, but a Communist government still holds control in Laos, which remains one of the poorest countries in East Asia.

Vietnam has maintained a sometimes difficult relationship with China. Once allies, the relationship between the two countries disintegrated after Vietnam signed a friendship pact with the Soviet Union in 1979. In deference to its new ally, the Vietnamese began driving out Chinese citizens who had settled in the North. Chinese military commanders, believing the Vietnamese army had been weakened because it had committed more than 100,000 troops to the conflict against the Khmer Rouge, sent 200,000 soldiers across the border. Entering Vietnam on February 17, the Chinese soldiers encountered heavy resistance. They got no further than the city of Lang Son, about 25 miles (40 km) south of the border. On March 16, the

Prisoners held by the Khmer Rouge had their clothing and other possessions confiscated.

Chinese withdrew.

After the skirmishes in 1979, the Vietnamese and Chinese were slow to resolve their differences. However, in 1991—after the fall of the Soviet Union and Vietnam's withdrawal from Cambodia—the two nations resumed trading with each other. In 2005, they expanded their economic ties when they permitted businesses to sign deals worth more than $1 billion. Still, the Vietnamese continue to watch China carefully. Each country lays claim to the oil-rich Spratly Islands in the South China Sea, and both maintain military outposts on the islands. By the late 2010s, China was investing heavily in Vietnam, but the relationship remains uneasy as the two continue to argue over which country has control of the South China Sea and other land near their borders.

Rebuilding and Unifying

While Vietnam's leaders struggled with their neighbors, they also worked to rebuild their country. The environment was terribly damaged, as jungles and agricultural lands alike had been burned by napalm (a substance used in flamethrowers and fire bombs) and defoliated by Agent Orange. Even now, some children born in Vietnam have birth defects that can be traced to the lingering effects of Agent Orange. The rate of cancer and other illnesses is also higher than in other parts of the world.

After the war, the Vietnamese needed new roads, utilities, homes, fuel, and most everything else. When journalist Peter T. White visited Hanoi in 1989, he found little progress had been made in the 14 years since the war's end. The Vietnamese economy was too weak to support the nation's people, and incomes were tiny. "To make ends meet, a doctor in charge of a hospital has had to be a janitor at night," he wrote. "A distinguished general in retirement must depend on his wife selling cigarettes in the street; she walks two miles a day so she won't have to lose face with the neighbors."[37]

Conditions would get even worse. After the war, the Vietnamese government had relied on the Soviet Union for economic aid. This aid dried up as the Soviet Union collapsed. Vietnam's economy went into a tailspin.

Following the Soviet downfall, however, the United States and Vietnam took their first tentative steps toward reconciliation. After the war ended in 1975, the United States had maintained a trade embargo against Vietnam, making it illegal for American companies to do business in the Asian country. However, in 1994, President Bill Clinton started removing those barriers. American corporations were allowed to invest in the country. The policy change also permitted Americans to visit the country. In 1995, Vietnam established an embassy in Washington, D.C. In 2004, journalist David Lamb, who had covered the Vietnam War in the 1960s and 1970s, returned to visit Hanoi. In describing the city, Lamb said it appeared that the Vietnamese had worked hard to put the war behind them:

> By breakfast time the sidewalks have been claimed by women in conical hats hawking vegetables and flowers, by vendors selling 20-cent bowls of lemon-grass-flavored chicken noodle soup known as pho ga—Hanoians will tell you their pho and bia (beer) are far superior to what is produced in Ho Chi Minh City—and by gaggles of motor scooters with nowhere else to park. Everyone is busy: sewing, welding, jackhammering, lugging, selling, cooking, repairing, sawing, building.[38]

Despite some improvements in their living conditions, the people of Vietnam face other hardships. In many ways, they must endure the repression that has long characterized Communist governments around the world. In Vietnam—as well as in China, Cuba, and other Communist countries—freedom of expression is stifled. Dissent is seldom tolerated. Electoral power is not held by the people. The government maintains tight control over the country's newspapers, radio stations, and television stations. Vietnamese citizens who have posted pro-democracy messages on the internet have been arrested.

In 2007, Vietnamese Prime Minister Nguyen Tan Dung hosted a chat session with his country's internet users. About 20,000 Vietnamese citizens sent messages to Dung during the 2-hour session. Some of the internet users questioned the lack of press freedom in Vietnam, while others complained about the government's seizure of private farmland. Dung generally defended the government's activities, but some citizens praised him for giving them a rare opportunity to question the government. Hanoi taxi driver Nguyen Trung Van told a reporter, "I don't know whether the issues we raised to our leaders will be addressed or not. But this is a good start because we need a channel to communicate with our leaders."[39]

As of 2019, North and South Vietnam are still at odds. Vietnamese journalist and author Huy Duc puts it this way: "No matter how strong our economy is, the conflict among Vietnamese people on both sides is still very strong … So the thing we have to do is not only unify the different parts of the country, but also unify people's hearts."[40]

The Powell Doctrine

The Vietnam War had a major effect on the U.S. military. In 1973, with no more need to conscript soldiers, President Nixon ended the draft. Since then, the U.S. military has been an all-volunteer force, relying on people who enlist because they want to serve. The number of American soldiers has shrunk dramatically since Vietnam. Partially, that is because the country does not currently need a large standing army. Partially, it is because automation and new technologies now handle jobs once performed by soldiers. Most experts agree the modern all-volunteer army is more effective. Morale is higher than in the Vietnam era, and soldiers enlist for longer service terms, so they are better trained.

What has also changed since Vietnam is the willingness of the American people to suffer casualties in a protracted ground war. During the 1980s and 1990s, numerous military and civilian leaders established criteria to be met before the United States would commit to military action. One of the most famous of these, as elaborated by General Colin Powell at the end of the 1991 Gulf War, is known as the Powell Doctrine.

Powell had served in Vietnam as a major and stayed in the military through the transition to an all-volunteer force. According to the Powell Doctrine, the United States would only commit forces in the case of a vital threat to national security, and only after all other means to find a peaceful solution had been exhausted. The United States was to exert overwhelming force to win a clear military victory, then retire from the battlefield without becoming involved in a Vietnam-style entanglement. In a 1992 essay in the journal *Foreign Affairs*, Powell explained, "We owe it to the men and women who go in harm's way to make sure that ... their lives are not squandered for unclear purposes."[41]

Throughout the 1990s, U.S. leaders followed this policy. In 1994, President Bill Clinton refused to send U.S. soldiers to intervene in the African nation of Rwanda, where more than 800,000 people were massacred in a systematic program of genocide. In 1999, Clinton ruled out the intervention of U.S. ground troops in Kosovo, a European country where a bloody civil war was being waged, although he did authorize high-altitude bombing and cruise missile strikes.

Invasion of Iraq

By 2003, George W. Bush was president, and the United States was struggling against Islamic fundamentalists who opposed American interests and threatened to wage war using terrorist tactics. Bush and his advisors feared that Saddam Hussein, the dictator of Iraq, possessed weapons of mass destruction and planned to sell them to terrorists. To stop him, in March 2003, the U.S. military invaded Iraq.

At first, Bush received considerable support from Congress and the American people. American troops easily swept aside the Iraqi military, captured Hussein, and installed a democratic government. However, the situation quickly deteriorated into a civil war as opposing religious factions battled for control of the country. Each day brought new reports of Iraqis killed in terrorist attacks, as well as endless infighting among the religious groups. American troops were targeted as well, as the insurgents wanted them out of the country. Like Vietnam, the Iraq War stretched into a long military campaign that eventually lost the support of

Saddam Hussein was a dictator who posed what many U.S. leaders believed was a threat to the United States. Because of this, U.S. troops were called to participate in a drawn-out war in Iraq.

A PERMANENT AND PORTABLE MEMORIAL

Each year, more than 4 million people visit the Vietnam Veterans Memorial in Washington, D.C. Dedicated in 1982, the memorial's main feature is a 246-foot (75 m) black granite wall. The names of nearly 60,000 American men and women who either died in Vietnam or remain missing in action are etched on this wall. Nearby is a statue depicting three weary American servicemen as they would have appeared during the height of the conflict. The statue, created by sculptor Frederick Hart, is known as *The Three Soldiers*.

The wall was designed by Maya Ying Lin, a Chinese American woman who was an architecture student at Yale University. She submitted the design as part of an open competition and won. At the time, the selection was controversial. Critics complained that a black wall would not adequately communicate the drama of the war. In response, the selection committee included *The Three Soldiers* statue as another way to commemorate the war. Racism also found its way into the controversy, as some critics suggested that a design submitted by a woman of Asian ethnicity was inappropriate because the war had pitted Asians against Americans. However, the committee dismissed such criticisms and stuck with Lin's design.

In addition to the permanent exhibit in Washington, the Vietnam Veterans Memorial Fund transports a smaller model of the wall, called *The Wall That Heals*, throughout the United States. That way, people across the nation have a chance to see it.

At the Vietnam Veterans Memorial in Washington, D.C., a long wall with the names of fallen soldiers is a sobering reminder of the human cost of the war.

most Americans.

Bush refused to pull out American troops before Iraq was stabilized. As a result, the war dragged on. By early 2007, more than 3,500 Americans had died in the conflict, often from sniper attacks or exploding roadside bombs.

Just as the atrocities of My Lai and the street executions of Viet Cong guerrillas had once horrified Americans, similar stories coming out of Iraq fueled public furor over the war. In late 2005, a squad of U.S. Marines was accused of murdering 24 unarmed Iraqi citizens in the town of Haditha, echoing the tragedy of My Lai. Shocking photographs and reports emerged about inhumane conditions at Abu Ghraib, a U.S. military prison in Iraq. When Congress convened hearings on the abuse of prisoners at Abu Ghraib, a stunned Senator John McCain—who had been tortured as a prisoner of war in North Vietnam—said, "I have seen a lot of people die. I've seen a lot of terrible things in my life. But to see it done by Americans to human beings is what's so appalling. It's so outrageous, I can't describe it."[42]

Over the years, many people have drawn comparisons between the Vietnam War and the war in Iraq. Just as Presidents Johnson and Nixon did not have any identifiable end goal for the Vietnam conflict, neither did President Bush and his administration more than 30 years later. There was no clear strategy on what to win, how to win it, or how to walk away. The enemy was underestimated because it was not clearly understood. In both Vietnam and Iraq, the Americans' enemies were willing to just keep fighting, no matter what, costing the United States money and lives.

There is little reason to think that wars will end. Instead, it is far more likely they will continue being fought across the planet, for one reason or another. Regardless of which country they live in or what side they are on, people can only hope that some lessons are being learned—and remembered.

Notes

Introduction: The Longest War

1. Quoted in American Presidency Project, University of California Santa Barbara, "Lyndon Johnson, Remarks to the International Platform Association upon Receiving the Association's Annual Award," August 3, 1965. www.presidency.ucsb.edu/ws/index.php?pid=27126.

2. Townsend Hoopes, "Legacy of the Cold War in Indochina," *Foreign Affairs*, July 1970, p. 609.

Chapter One: The Search for Independence

3. Lyn Reese, "The Trung Sisters," Women in World History Curriculum, accessed on September 4, 2018. www.womeninworldhistory.com/heroine10.html.

4. Quoted in Marilyn B. Young, *The Vietnam Wars*. New York, NY: HarperPerennial, 1991, p. 3.

5. Quoted in Geoff Simons, *Vietnam Syndrome: Impact on U.S. Foreign Policy*. New York, NY: St. Martin's Press, 1998, p. 88.

6. Quoted in American Experience, "Vietnam Online," PBS, accessed on September 5, 2018. www.shoppbs.pbs.org/wgbh/amex/vietnam/series/pt_01.html.

7. Quoted in American Experience, "Vietnam Online."

Chapter Two: Spreading and Expanding

8. Quoted in John Corry, "TV: 13-Part History of Vietnam War on PBS," *New York Times*, 1983. www.nytimes.com/1983/10/04/movies/tv-13-part-history-of-vietnam-war-on-pbs.html.

9. Quoted in Stanley Karnow, *Vietnam: A History*. New York, NY: Penguin, 1997, p. 429.

10. Quoted in American Experience, "Vietnam Online."

11. Quoted in Young, *The Vietnam Wars*, p. 144.

12. Quoted in Young, *The Vietnam Wars*, p. 210.

13. Quoted in Young, *The Vietnam Wars*, p. 215.

14. Quoted in American Experience, "Vietnam Online."

15. Quoted in Young, *The Vietnam Wars*, p. 217.

16. Michael D. Mosettig, "The Campaign that Changed how Americans Saw the Vietnam War," PBS, January 31, 2018. www.pbs.org/newshour/world/the-campaign-that-changed-how-americans-saw-the-vietnam-war.

Chapter Three: A Time of Protest

17 . Martin Luther King Jr., "This Madness Must Cease," Centre for Research of Globalization. www.globalresearch.ca/index.php?context=viewArticle&code=%20KI20070115&articleId=4460.

18. Abbie Hoffman, *Soon to Be a Major Motion Picture*. New York, NY: Berkley, 1982, p. 151.

19. Richard Goldstein, "Hugh Thompson, 62, Who Saved Civilians at My Lai, Dies." *New York Times*, January 7, 2006. www.nytimes.com/2006/01/07/us/hugh-thompson-62-who-saved-civilians-at-my-lai-dies.html.

20. Quoted in Michael Bilton and Kevin Sim, *Four Hours in My Lai*. New York, NY: Viking Penguin, 1992, p. 219.

21. Quoted in Michael Maclear, *The Ten Thousand Day War: Vietnam, 1945–1975*. New York, NY: St. Martin's, 1981, p. 275.

22. John McCain and Mark Salter, *Faith of My Fathers: A Family Memoir*. New York, NY: Random House, 1999, pp. 242–243.

23. McCain and Salter, *Faith of My Fathers*, p. 345.

Chapter Four: Talk of Peace

24. Jason Daley, "Notes Indicate Nixon Interfered with 1968 Peace Talks," *Smithsonian*, January 2, 2017. www.smithsonianmag.com/smart-news/notes-indicate-nixon-interfered-1968-peace-talks-180961627/.

25. Quoted in Karnow, *Vietnam*, p. 597.

26. Quoted in Maclear, *The Ten Thousand Day War*, p. 260.

27. Quoted in Young, *The Vietnam Wars*, p. 238.

28. Quoted in Karnow, *Vietnam*, p. 592.

29. Quoted in Young, *The Vietnam Wars*, p. 271.

30. Quoted in American Experience, "Vietnam Online."

Chapter Five: Broken Promises

31. Quoted in Bob Woodward and Carl Bernstein, *All the President's Men*. New York, NY: Warner, 1975, p. 26.

32. Quoted in American Experience, "Vietnam Online."

33. Quoted in American Experience, "Vietnam Online."

34. Phillip B. Davidson, *Vietnam at War: The History, 1946–1975*. Novato, CA: Presidio, 1988, p. 769.

35. Quoted in Maclear, *The Ten Thousand Day War*, p. 342.

36. Quoted in American Experience, "Vietnam Online."

Epilogue: Lessons Learned

37. Peter T. White, "Vietnam: Hard Road to Peace," *National Geographic*, November 1989, p. 570.

38. David Lamb, "Hanoi: Shedding the Ghosts of War," *National Geographic*, May 2004, p. 80.

39. Quoted in Margie Mason, "Vietnam's Leader Goes to the People—Online," *Philadelphia Inquirer*, February 10, 2007, p. A-4.

40. Thomas Maresca, "40 Years Later, Vietnam Still Deeply Divided Over War," *USA Today*, April 30, 2015. www.usatoday.com/story/news/world/2015/04/28/fall-of-saigon-vietnam-40-years-later/26447943/.

41. Colin Powell, "US Forces: The Challenges Ahead." *Foreign Affairs*, Winter 1992–1993, p. 32.

42. Quoted in Sheryl Gay Stolberg, "Prisoner Abuse Scandal Puts McCain in Spotlight Once Again," *New York Times*, May 10, 2004, p. A-19.

For More Information

Books

Atwood, Kathryn. *Courageous Women of the Vietnam War: Medics, Journalists, Survivors, and More.* Chicago, IL: Chicago Review Press, 2018.
> This book focuses on the roles women assumed during the Vietnam War, including jobs as nurses and journalists.

The Vietnam War: The Definitive Illustrated History. New York, NY: DK Publishing, 2017.
> Produced in conjunction with the Smithsonian Institution, this book is made up of highly informational spreads of photographs.

Diggs, Barbara. *The Vietnam War.* White River Junction, VT: Nomad Press, 2018.
> This book for young adults explores the global conditions that led to the Vietnam War and includes information such as speeches, letters, and photographs.

Freedman, Russell. *Vietnam: A History of the War.* New York, NY: Holiday House, 2016.
> Readers can get an overview of the conflict, as well as view historic photos. Extensive research materials are provided for students to further explore.

Sheinkin, Steve. *Most Dangerous: Daniel Ellsberg and the Secret History of the Vietnam War.* New York, NY: Roaring Brook Press, 2015.
> This book looks closely at the man who leaked the Pentagon Papers, his reasons for doing it, and how it impacted the Vietnam War and the American public.

Websites

Embassy of Vietnam
vietnamembassy-usa.org
>Visitors to the Embassy of Vietnam's website can read news about the country and learn about Vietnamese culture. The website includes 26 lessons in the Vietnamese language.

Lyndon B. Johnson
www.lbjlib.utexas.edu
>The website maintained by the Lyndon Baines Johnson Library and Museum at the University of Texas in Austin includes many online resources, including copies of speeches given by Johnson, an archive of photographs, images from the president's daily diary, and audio and video clips of the former president.

The Vietnam War
www.pbs.org/kenburns/the-vietnam-war/home/?utm_source=WeAreTeachers&utm_campaign=vietnamwar_2017&utm_medium=web
>This PBS television series is considered one of the most authoritative and fascinating resources for all ages. Information about episodes and stories share space with lessons and primary resources.

Vietnam War History
www.history.com/topics/vietnam-war/vietnam-war-history
>This website offers a thorough history of the Vietnam War, including its causes, major events during the war, and its aftermath. Several photo collections are included.

"The War in Vietnam: A Story in Photographs"
www.archives.gov/education/lessons/vietnam-photos
>Each photograph in this collection from the National Archives leads to further lessons and documents from the time period.

Index

Dong, Pham Van, 16
Dong Xoai, 32
draft, 31, 42–43, 60, 89
drugs, 62
Duc, Huy, 89
Dung, Nguyen Tan, 89
Dung, Van Tien, 78–79
dysentery, 54, 56

E
Ellsberg, Daniel, 67, 74
Eisenhower, Dwight D., 18, 60
Europe, 9, 11–12, 22, 90

F
Fenwick, Millicent, 78
Fink, Charles, 30
First Indochina War, 6, 16, 18, 56
Fonda, Jane, 42
fragging, 71
France, 11–12, 15–18, 64
friendly fire, 71

G
Gallup poll, 42, 51
Geneva Conventions, 56
Geneva, Switzerland, 6, 18
genocide, 62, 64, 90
Germany, 12
Grant Park, 46–47
Great Britain, 11–12, 15
Gulf of Tonkin Resolution, 6, 23–24, 42
Gulf War, 90

H
Haditha, 92
Haiphong, 16, 69, 72
Haldeman, H. R., 58, 60

Hanoi, 15–18, 56–57, 72, 88–89
Harrington, Myron, 40
Hart, Frederick, 93
helicopters, 34, 48, 50, 77, 79
hepatitis C, 52
Hmong, 64
Ho Chi Minh Trail, 14, 18, 28, 30, 63, 76
Hoffman, Abbie, 46–47
Hoopes, Townsend, 10
Hope, Bob, 66
House Armed Services Committee, 49
Hue, 20, 36, 38, 40, 78
Humphrey, Hubert, 35, 58–59
Huong, Tran Van, 79
Hussein, Saddam, 90–91

I
infections, 54
Iraq, 66, 90, 92

J
Japan, 6, 12, 15
Johnson, Lyndon B., 9, 23–24, 27–29, 31–32, 35, 40–41, 46, 58–59, 67, 93

K
Karnow, Stanley, 19
Kennedy, John F., 21, 23
Kent State University, 51
Khe Sanh, 36
Khmer Rouge, 64, 84, 86–87
King, Martin Luther, Jr., 43
Kissinger, Henry, 67, 71, 74, 76
Korean War, 17, 40, 60, 66
Kosovo, 90

Picture Credits

Cover, pp. 34, 37, 61 Tim Page/CORBIS/Corbis via Getty Images; pp. 6 (left), 7 (middle), 35, 59 courtesy of the National Archives; p. 6 (middle) Jean-Claude LABBE/Gamma-Rapho via Getty Images; pp. 6 (right), 24 MPI/Getty Images; pp. 7 (left), 80–81 nik wheeler/Corbis via Getty Images; p. 7 (right) Hoang Dinh Nam/Pool/Getty Images; pp. 6–7 (background), 26 Eye Ubiquitous/ UIG via Getty Images; p. 8 pavalena/Shutterstock.com; p. 13 KEYSTONE-FRANCE/Gamma-Rapho via Getty Images; p. 14 ADN-Bildarchiv/ullstein bild via Getty Images; p. 15 jorisvo/Shutterstock.com; p. 17 Hung Chung Chih/ Shutterstock.com; p. 19 beibaoke/Shutterstock.com ; pp. 21 (both), 22, 38, 49, 52, 54–55, 57, 65, 68, 77 Bettmann/Getty Images; p. 23 Edumund J. Fitzgerald/Naval History and Heritage Command/Navy.mil; p. 27 official USMC photo by Lance Corporal W. R. Schaaf; pp. 28–29 Air Force Historical Support Division/U.S. Air Force; pp. 31, 47 Hulton Archive/Getty Images; p. 33 Dominique BERRETTY/Gamma-Rapho via Getty Images; p. 39 Robert Alexander/Getty Images; pp. 44–45 Harold Adler/Underwood Archives/Getty Images; p. 51 Steven Clevenger/Corbis via Getty Images; p. 63 Akane1988/Shutterstock.com; p. 66 Silver Screen Collection/ Getty Images; p. 70 Sovfoto/UIG via Getty Images; p. 72 AFP/Getty Images; p. 75 courtesy of the Library of Congress; p. 82 John Bill/Shutterstock.com; p. 85 MPI/Getty Images; p. 87 Hulton-Deutsch Collection/CORBIS/Corbis via Getty Images; p. 91 Pierre PERRIN/Gamma-Rapho via Getty Images; p. 92 Sean Pavone/ Shutterstock.com.

About the Author

Tamra B. Orr is the author of more than 500 nonfiction and educational books for readers of all ages. She graduated from Ball State University in Muncie, Indiana, with a degree in English and Education. She planned on becoming an English teacher. Instead, she moved to Oregon and began writing books. She is old enough to remember the draft for the Vietnam War and the names of young men scrolling on the television. She recalls watching the list carefully for her older brother's name and taking a deep breath every time she did not see it.